# THRASHER
## INSANE TERRAIN

UNIVERSE

**THRASHER**

**Previous Spread:** Mr. Incredible, Ty Page goes Double Live Gonzo on the Firestone demo ramp before humpteen thousand heshers at Cal Jam II in the Cali wasteland, 1977.

First published in the United States of America in 2001
by UNIVERSE PUBLISHING
A Division of Rizzoli International Publications, Inc.
300 Park Avenue South
New York, NY 10010

©2001 Universe Publishing
Photographs © High Speed Productions, Inc.

01 02 03 04 / 10 9 8 7 6 5 4 3 2 1

Library of Congress Catalog Number:

Editor: Terence Maikels
Designers: Vincent Arnone and Edward Brogna

Printed in Hong Kong

*Insane Terrain* is dedicated to Phil Shao, Ruben Orkin and Curtis Hsiang, three skateboarders who gave and got everything they could when called to ride. May they ride on.

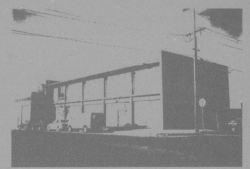

**INSANE TERRAIN**

Terrain is where you find it. Ped X-ing bling bling, Anytown, USA.

"It all started . . ." Lawrence John Hitch III and his skateboard. The perfect vehicle, just when you needed it most.

# INTRODUCTION

The stories are always there, it just takes a book to make sure they get written. The reason for the existence of this book is to pass along a part of the story of the skateboard and those who ride them. Anybody who has spent time amongst a dedicated group of skateboarders realizes they have a different way of looking at the world. A different agenda. It's all about the terrain. Skateboarders study and accept the terrain and the architecture that has been placed upon it like no other human beings. Skateboarders are not want for past or future because they are always in the now. "Is it skateable, can we skate it?" Skaters study the curbline from the car as they drive by on the street, drawing a route that hits every inflection, curb cut, crack, and ollie nub along the way. Benches and blocks that go unsat-upon by the few pedestrians rushing by are slid, ground, relished, and appreciated by roving skaters. Steps are to be cleared on the fly and nine will get you ten. You go back to the schoolyard on Saturday mornings to skate the playground banks. There are still enough old schoolers around to make the question "Got any empty pools?" a far better proposition than any drug deal. That skater coming at you down the sidewalk may end up a friend for life.

Skateboarders are certainly not above the classes of nerd, loner, freak, or kook, as everyone is prone to fall into on occasion. But when these varied walks meet in a skate space, look out! Nowhere else will you find a more diverse yet talented group of individuals. Skaters may not have played team sports, joined a gang, or even gone to church. Yet, skaters have infiltrated and influenced art, architecture and music in the same way they would "thrash" a fresh new skate spot. And they know how to fix your car and hook up your stereo.

*Insane Terrain* is not only a celebration of twenty years of *Thrasher* magazine, but a hail to the spirit and adventure of skateboarding, the spots that are legendary, the skateboarders who have sought them out and the innovators that continue to pusue the basic rush of finding it and sticking it.

Nowhere is the embodiment of the skate spirit found more than in the person of Jake Phelps, *Thrasher* editor for the last ten years. Jake continues to search, seek, and question everything that a skateboard has to offer even as he cracks his body one more time in the pursuit. Generally speaking, Jake has been there and has done it.

If there is a model for this book, other than the pages of *Thrasher*, it would be *National Geographic* magazine. Our intention is to present a clear, awe-inspiring picture into the world of the skaters and the terrain they ride. A collection of photographs that will confound the clueless, wow the masses, and inspire those who would go where no one else has ever been. Flip through this book, look at the pictures, read the captions. This book is not a how-to manual, you'll sort of have to figure that out on your own, and it does not contain any safety precautions, rules, regulations, glossaries of terms, or skatepark lists. Skate safe today, skate again tomorrow, don't stay in one spot too long, and seek and you shall find are about the only advice we will offer in those areas. There are some classic tales and anecdotes to read if you want to go there. Some of the stories, interviews, and editorials from the pages of *Thrasher* magazine have been condensed and edited or updated to fit the context of the times. Photos were chosen to represent a timeless depiction of a skater, at a spot, that connects with all of those who have experienced it or want it.

—Kevin Thatcher, May 2001

**Following Spread:** "I remember we took my sister's roller skates and mounted them on a two-by-four. . . ." One day, possibly long before this "anything on wheels" derby happened on New York City's East Side in 1952, some kid crashed his skate crate into a tree, and wobbled off down the hill on just a plank with four wheels. The rest is history.

"Find, grind, and leave it behind." Barefootin' rebel pool raider floats through the deep end of a West L.A. bowl in the early 1960s. Although designed for a swim, an empty swimming pool offered the skater "natural" transitions and the freedom of expression afforded by a "magic rolling board." A skater does not trash the terrain that is skated upon, but rather recycles it and makes it live again.

# HISTORY OF SKATEBOARDING

The history of skateboarding is as old as the invention of the wheel and as recent as yesterday's session. The skateboard is an icon that is recognized by most, much maligned by a few, and embraced by a cult of enlightened thrill seekers and daredevils who have tapped in to the magic and energy of a plank with four wheels under it. Skateboarding has a rich history charged with youthful intensity and adventurous spirit, while the skateboard itself has changed very little in concept and design.

In America, modern skateboard riding and the mass production of ready-to-skate equipment has been around for over forty years and continues to show every intention of being around for hundreds more. It's hard to find anyone whose been livin' in the USA during this period, skater or not, who doesn't have a story to tell or a board in their closet. Product development and skating styles coincided with the invention and perfection of two other modern American postwar activities: Surfing and suburban sprawl. Somewhere in between a growing population of waveless "valleys" and landlocked surfers, skateboarders multiplied to fill in the cracks created by a coast-to-coast pour of asphalt and cement that continues to this day. With arguably one less wave breaking everyday and endless flows of streets and sidewalks and parking lots covering the landscape, skateboarding was a natural way to gain a toehold as a favorite pastime pleasure for fun-seeking grommets with energy to burn.

Speaking of cracks and toes, the first sidewalk surfers who pushed off down the driveways of Southern California and through beachside parking lots in Florida on a pine plank mounted with their sister's purloined metal-wheeled roller-skate set-ups did so barefoot and were routinely pitched headlong from their sticks upon encountering the slightest crack or strewn pebble. Horrified parents, convinced that skateboarding was just another equivalent for falling out of trees and stupid stuff they did as youngsters, quickly dubbed skateboarding as dangerous, while their kids invented new scabs and knew that skateboarding was the coolest thing in the world.

The dawn of skateboarding coincided with the realization of the industrial revolution in America and the increase in cheaper mass-production of steel products for car parts, tools, and toys. Ancestors of the skateboard would include the Radio Flyer wagon, two-wheeled scooters (borrowing from bicycle technology), the Flexi Flyer (a snow sled with four wheels), three- and four-wheeled pushcarts of every description, mostly homemade using a wooden packing crate body mounted on a wood frame chassis riding on old lawnmower wheels fastened with a crude steel axle and cotter pin system. All of these vehicles were suitable for pushing, pulling, coasting, and bombing the nearest hill run and all had a front-wheel, hand- or foot-operated steering system.

The real matriarch of this radical toy family, though, was the roller skate, which has been around since the early 1800s and by the early part of the twentieth century were mostly manufactured by Roller Sports, Inc. of Chicago. Early skates featured steel wheels riding on ball bearings around axles that were mounted so they would pivot at an angle to the base plates, which were attached to a hard-soled skate boot. This pivoting action allowed for turning maneuverability by leaning the body and legs from side to side to go left or right, while the four wheels of each skate stayed on the ground. It wasn't long before backyard mechanics (dads) began mounting a set of wheels from one skate boot to the underside of a narrow wood plank topped with a fruit crate up front and a crosspiece for handlebars to create a crude version of the scooter. The day that some kid was bombing a hill, crashed into a tree that separated the handlebars, and continued on down balancing on just a plank with four wheels underneath is the day the skateboard was invented.

While there is physical evidence to support the existence of skateboards and skate scooters as early as the 1920s, the skate technology was in place 100 years before. It's possible that some little gnarler was pushing off on a skateboard in the late 1800s if he could find a smooth enough sidewalk at all. Regardless of when the first skateboard was actually conceived and ridden, the roller skate equipment that made it work stayed pretty much the same until the late 1950s. The only advancement in equipment would have been the clay/composite wheels developed for the wooden floors of indoor roller skate rinks, which gained popularity in the 1920s. The putty-colored "clay" wheels were smoother rolling, offered more stability than the steel wheels, and may have been mounted to a scooter or board, but the vehicle wasn't called a "skateboard" until the surfers got hold of them in the late 1940s and 1950s.

The surfers along the Southern California coast, at hot spots like Malibu, Santa Monica, Doheny, Huntington, and La Jolla Shores, were a close-knit fabric of nomadic beach dwellers, sitting astride a new sport that would soon carve its own niche and influence the world in many ways with music (Ventures and the Beach Boys) and fashion (baggy shorts and t-shirts) beyond the waves. During long summer flat spells with no rideable swells on the horizon, it was only natural that landbound surfers would revive and reinvent the skateboard, named after their favorite water toy. Roller skate set-ups were still the obvious choice, but two-by-four and plank sticks were starting to take shape. Influential surf pioneers like Mickey Dora, John Fries, and Squeak Blank were also amongst the first sidewalk surfers to carve down the coastal hillside grids of Pacific Palisades and Santa Monica, riding smoother streets and driveways all the way to the beach parking lots of Malibu and Venice on surf-inspired skateboard shapes with rounded noses and tails.

By the late 1950s surfing had a toehold on a baby boom–bred youth movement that was also fueling interest in hot rods, motorcycles, and rock and roll. The late 1950s saw the introduction of the first factory-produced Little Red Roller Derby, stamped steel wheels and trucks riveted on a bullet-shaped 19″ x 4 1/2″ plywood board with barely an inch of nose or tail. By the early 1960s other roller skate and toy manufacturers had followed the fad. Nash Manufacturing out of Fort Worth, Texas, produced a 22″ long solid wood, steel-wheeled Sidewalk Surfboard. These toy boards

brought sidewalk surfing to the landlocked Midwest and subdivided communities of single family dwellings spreading out between the coasts.

By the time Beach Boys soundalikes Jan and Dean released their hit "Bust your Buns (And Go Sidewalk Surfin' With Me)" in 1964, skateboarding was a true fad that was selling millions of units and sweeping the nation alongside youth crazes like the Hula Hoop. Surf industry pioneers like Hobie Alter and Dewey Weber licensed their names to adorn oak and laminated surfboard-shaped decks using the more sidewalk friendly clay wheels and double-action trucks that pivoted on two rubber bushings. Hobie even introduced a wider fiberglass deck that featured a low-slung rocker design and clay "coconut" white Super Surfer wheels, hinting at the possibility of skateboard-specific leanings in design and technology. Early complete boards with surf-style graphics were advertised in surf mags, and shop teams and contests sprung up.

During the mid 1960s a brief boom flared and "sidewalk surfin'" was the call; however, the standard roller skate technology and clay wheels remained static, impeding the skater from any great progress. The majority of skateboard sales were still toy boards from the toy and variety stores, and the 'fad' faded. Skateboarding shrunk back to the coasts in the late 1960s as other influences like the British pop invasion (Beatles) and changing social concerns (Vietnam, drugs) swept the nation. However, the seeds had been planted, and while many skateboards were being retired to hang on garage rafters, there was still new cement and asphalt being poured every day.

The boom/bust cycle has occurred a number of times in skateboarding's brief history. In 1974 there appeared a catalyst that vaulted skateboarding into the modern era as an activity that was so dynamic as to influence several generations of youthful participants. The urethane wheel literally transformed things overnight.

The big roller skate companies had been experimenting with a plastic and urethane skate wheel since the late 1950s. The new compounds were rejected by the indoor rink crowd as too slow on the smooth hard wood, and any benefit of traction was lost on the tame hand-holding and figure-skating style of the day. Around 1974, some wily surf/skaters who had kept their clay-wheeled Super Surfers

oiled during the down time discovered these urethane wheels designed for roller skates, slapped them under their boards, and skateboarding literally took off. The new wheel allowed skaters to move beyond the simple carves of earlier generations and suddenly radical slalom, downhill street, poolriding, and skating in spillways and drainage ditches came to prominence. No longer would the smallest crack or pebble stop and launch a skater off their board. Familiar skate wheel makers like Roller Sports and Metaflex dominated the market at first with urethane cut from the same molds as the clay wheels and riding on eight loose ball bearings per side, sixteen per wheel.

Frank Nasworthy is generally given credit for his revelation in bringing urethane wheels down to a group of surf/skate rats on the beaches of San Diego, and soon the "Cadillac Kid" Greg Weaver and shooting stars like Ty Page and Mike Weed were carving vertical walls in pools on skateboard magazine covers, announcing a new era in skateboarding's history. Old-school pros like Tom Sims, Torger Johnson, and the Logan Brothers took to the streets to revive a slalom and freestyle scene. Meanwhile, up in the pool-rich neighborhoods around Santa Monica and West L.A., and down around the beaches and neighborhoods of Venice, the skaters who had never stopped during the drought years took the new freedom afforded by urethane to unseen new levels and reset the rule book on skateboarding. The clear red Road Rider Wheel distributed by NHS/ Santa Cruz locked in the possibilities with the unique precision bearing, two per wheel, which did as much for the glide as urethane did for the ride. These two developments allowed skateboarders to explore new radical heights every day. Skateboarding became an adventure and ultimately a lifestyle for many wayward youth gone wild. Nothing else mattered. To keep up with explosive advancements by the skaters, product development kicked into high gear: boards, wheels and trucks made with every material known in all shapes and sizes. Some worked, most didn't. The cream rose to the top, and skateboard-specific companies run by skateboarders began to replace the old roller skate monopolies. Many of the proven concepts from this industrious era are still the standards by which all are measured today.

After the Road Rider revolution, everyone made a clear red wheel, and by 1976 the precision bearing was standard in most wheels. Urethane was refined another notch with the Sims Competition wheel that was bigger and more resilient and lively for greater speeds on smooth pools and the skateboard parks that began appearing everywhere. Tunnel Rocks one-upped the Sims wheel with the same square profile but improved urethane, and then manufacturers like Kryptonics and Gyro started trimming wheel fat with radial (round) and conical (angled) edges. Every size, shape, and combination was being offered. Wizard wheels had tread like a car tire, Z-Grooves featured … you guessed it. Emotion wheels had urethane over the bearings and rubber on the outer edge. G&S Rollerballs were totally round, like riding on four golf balls. Starbrites had lights that would flash on when they rolled. Wheels had metal and plastic cores, came in sizes and shapes of every description, urethane colors in every hue and hardness.

Trucks like Excaliber, Sure Grip, and Chicago were still basically roller skate trucks adapted for skateboards, with axles threaded all the way across to accommodate the old loose ball and cone wheel systems. Trackers appeared and were wider and stronger but sluggish. Bennett trucks were lighter and snappier, turning with a smooth axle under the bearings, but the plastic base plates cracked easily and

**Facing Page and This Page:** While skateboarders may have borrowed the crude pivot-action truck and axle steering system from roller skate technology, they added a hard surf-styled stance and quickly adapted it to a mode and coda of their own. The sidewalk became the preferred playground and the streets were for free. This suburban Santa Monica, CA, crew posing for a commercial shoot in 1959 had it down, from bun bustin' to band-aids . . . and the chicks dug it.

they were hard to come by. Base plates went from narrow four-hole bolt patterns to wider three-hole, then back to the wider four-hole that is still common today. Skateboard trucks that worked still retained the same basic principles and upright geometry borrowed from roller skating. There were attempts at all manner of "improvements" to the skateboard truck using springs, two sets of bushings, and kingpins set at pivot angles with the adjustment nut sticking out the front of the hanger. Variflex actually did this with success. Toy giant Mattel tried to reinvent wheels and trucks as part of their Magnum system, but it was so overpriced and nonfunctional that skaters just laughed. The first Gullwings were angled trucks with split axles, multiple bushings, and adjustments for stiffness and turning radius. They were useless for grinding and quickly redesigned to the standards of the day. The Hobie Sundancer was a full skateboard with only two wheels; imagine a steamroller. It rolled in a straight line but as soon as you tried to turn, it got ugly. Z Products were always on the creative edge, and their Z-Roller truck featured a rolling pin mounted over the axle so you rolled instead of ground. Stroker trucks were the most advanced and craziest trucks ever designed and built, using technology borrowed from the rack and pinion steering of a car, each wheel turning independently of the other. They worked for street carving and were stable at high speed, winning the "skate car" division of the Signal Hill, Long Beach downhill speed event. Independent trucks first appeared dominating slalom racing when they featured true independent suspension for each wheel, utilizing a square steel torsion bar and offset axles. Independent dropped the suspension idea for the street and vert market and developed a low-centered, stable and responsive truck that became the standard by which all others measured up to or stole ideas from.

There have always been wood boards, first of pine plank and two-by-four lumber, then solid hardwoods like oak and maple. As with wheels and trucks, however, the board boom of the 1970s saw every kind of material and shape idea put to the test. Since flex was thought to be important to skateboard performance, fiberglass was popular. Aluminum was light and strong enough so several companies tried it. The Banzai was a 24" aluminum board with pointed kicktails at each end—a shape of things to come? One of the biggest-selling skateboards in history was the GT by Grentec, a 20" plastic toy board with pot metal trucks and misshapen urethane wheels that many skaters actually had to claim as their first. The original Zephyr and later Z-Flex boards were fiberglass replicas of the Hobie "spoon" rocker of the 1960s; later the Hobie Park Rider was a low "dropped" center design. Camber is the opposite of rocker, and the slalom set used hump-backed flexible cambered boards to pump and speed carve into oblivion. Guys like Henry Hester and Bob Skoldberg were slalom kings on cambered fiberglass and wood ply slalom laminates until Tony Alva came out one day and blew them away on a solid oak Logan Torger Johnson model. Hmmm.

The kicktail was a major innovation, and arguments still rage over who invented it. There was a fiberglass deck called the Wayne Brown kicktail in 1975, but Larry Stephenson of Makaha skateboards claimed to have the patent on the kicktail. Plastic boards had molded kicktails, solid wood boards used a glued-on wedge, and eventually Santa Cruz, always at the forefront of the ply movement, pressed their popular five-ply with a kicktail, not much different in construction than (double kick) model boards of today. When side-to-side concave appeared, Santa Cruz Bevels took plywood board presses to the limit with a deep dish concave from the tail through the nose. Wide boards came out of Dogtown with Wes Humpston's personalized, hand-drawn 12" wide 'pigs' for him and Jim Muir, who were big boys who needed big boards. Alva was riding 10"-plus at the time. Kryptonics made a board out of foam laminated

between P-tex layers with a rubber bumper around the edge for protection. The Krypto board was light, stiff, and three times the price of other decks. G&S and Caster Fiberlams had good pop that went dead before the board did. The Santa Cruz Stinger and Haut Lamaflex used a double cutaway design from in front of the back truck through the rear wheels.

Accessories came and went as fast as anything. The first use of griptape was a piece of carpet or sandpaper glued to the deck. Later, skaters discovered a 3M adhesive-backed plastic safety tread at the hardware store. Skate shops started to get the real stuff later on, and even then some of the Badlands locals around Upland swore by "pizza deck," blood-red-colored super adhesive with razor-sharp gravel embedded in it—originally developed for sanding hardwood floors—that would cut to the touch. The first Tracker trucks came with wooden risers. Rad Pad risers were wedge-shaped, black rubber pads that changed the angle of the truck pivot when installed, making it turn more or less. There were plastic tail pivots and skids, rails and Nose Bones for boardslides and grabs, lappers and no hang devices for reentries, Copers and Grindmasters for smoother grinds and truck protection, and Sky Hooks attached to the top of a board as a hands-free air aid when you locked your feet in, as did the velcro straps of the short-lived Suspenders.

Throughout the 1970s, there were contests of many descriptions and disciplines. California Freeformer, Cadillac Nationals, and the Long Beach Pro/Am featured slalom, freestyle, barrel, and high jumping. Magic Mountain had a contest with a timed cross-country course. Catalina Classic was a Grand Prix–style downhill through the streets of Avalon. The legendary Signal Hill Downhill in Long Beach was a straight drop downhill drag race that was also described as a bloodbath, featuring stand up, lay down, and skate car divisions. All of these contests featured a healthy turnout in the women's division. There were halfpipe demos at major events like Cal Jam II and the Long Beach Grand Prix. At the height of the hype, a show called Skateboard Mania featuring some of the top pros of the day in costume toured arenas. Skateboarding's answer to the Ice Follies only lasted a few shows but did feature the Loop of Life.

The latter half of the 1970s saw skateboarding explode and create its own social register apart from the surf scene. The boom also coincided with an explosion in music called punk rock. Kids were listening to Ted Nugent one day, AC/DC the next, and the Sex Pistols and the Clash the week after that. Hair, clothing, and language changed daily, with skateboarders leading the charge at school and on the mall. Skateboarding welcomed all, from metalheads and stoners to outlaws and the outcast; even jocks and preps couldn't resist. Nerds and geeks who didn't play team sports found theirs in skateboarding and the do-it-yourself freedoms and friendships that it offered. Skateboarding cut across social boundaries like no other, and if you saw someone else with a board, no words needed to be spoken—you were bros. Still, for most non-skating civilians and pedestrians, the typical "skater dude" was Sean Penn's classic character Spicoli in the movie *Fast Times at Ridgemont High*, a typecast that is still hanging around.

Skateboard-specific companies stepped up their promotion and advertising campaigns, making substantial investments outside of just production costs. Touring pro skaters wandered the U.S. and Europe. By the late 1970s, massive skateboard parks were opening faster than the cement could dry. Pool contests were a natural order, and the mega parks of California were a proving ground. Henry Hester put together a pro poolriding series in 1977 that showcased the talents of the top vertical pros in the park pools of Upland Pipeline, Big O, Spring Valley, Oasis, and Del Mar. Winchester Skatepark in San Jose installed a perfect keyhole pool that featured some classic NorCal vs. SoCal

**Top:** Micke Alba returned to the Upland Pipeline one day to relive the glory days and launch out of the pipe on his old Krypstik.

**Center:** The origins of slash dog style. Tony Altieri works a low-pivotal rotation out of the slot formed by a Southern California reservoir circa 1976.

**Bottom:** Swedish punk rock skater mixes plaid with his DP stripes for an aggro loading dock drop.

Former famous Playboy Bunny Barbi Benton scoots around the studio lot during production of the ABC-TV series *Sugar*, in which she costarred as Maxx, a rock singer in an aspiring girl group.

showdowns. These bowl contests gave skaters a chance to prove themselves and showcase new radical moves. Stacy Peralta's vertical boardslides. Tay Hunt's high-speed cess-slides way past vertical in Upland's fullpipe. Salba's stalled tail blocks on coping. Sometimes a new trick could win a contest outright. Bobby Valdez did the first invert at a contest. Tim Marting showcased the rock 'n' roll. Blackhart simply rolled out and back in, over coping … frontside.

Skateboards had survived from the ashes of the 1970s and surely would be around to remember the 1980s. The 1980s dawned and many said skateboarding was dead. A few punkers still carried their boards to clubs, mercenaries still gathered to hand-bail a pool, and most of the big commercial parks were still standing, but only a dedicated group of locals, pros, and BMXers showed up for the evening sessions. The tide had changed on another sidewalk surf session—for now....

It may be that the demise of skateboarding began in the parks it had been relegated to. Of over 200 skateparks built in America in the 1970s, ninety percent were pay-to-play facilities that charged skaters to walk behind a fence and don the required helmet, wrist guards, elbow, and knee pads to skate on terrain that was sometimes so kinked and poorly designed as to be dangerous. Many experienced skaters decided they'd rather go back and skate the abandoned hotel pool down the street for free. Beginners were intimidated by the thought of dropping into a 12-foot-deep pool with four feet of vert or a downhill halfpipe with no flat bottom. Paramount skatepark's Vertibowl was 17-feet deep. Upland featured an 18-foot pipe with a 12-foot bowl and a 15-foot bowl at the end of a huge banked slalom run, and later installed the famous Combi-pool with its 12-foot round pool and 14-foot square rimmed with fat chunky coping.

The 1980s broke out pretty flat, but the skate sessions that were happening lacked not in intensity nor talent. A fairly healthy pro scene still thrived in the greater Southern California grid and those hardy crowds who witnessed the Gold Cup Series events from 1980–82 saw three of the greatest skateboarders ever in the prime of their careers. Eddie "El Gato" Elguera, Stevie Caballero, and Duane Peters, "The Master of Disaster," served up a rivalry with heated sessions that burned through Upland Pipeline's Combi, Skate City Whittier's keyhole, and the pools at Marina del Rey and Del Mar Skateranch. There was a kid in the amateur division spinning 540 units just below tile at the end of his run—I think his name was Tony Hawk—and Christian Hosoi was skating the little brown pools at Marina everyday while he waited for his ride across town. Like many skaters of the period, each had their own signature style: "Elguerials" had to be seen to be believed; "Caballerials" showed everyone what the ollie was for; and Duane was just being "Duurwaane" when he started his run with an acid drop to the deepest part of the bowl. Tony Hawk ollied to four feet, grabbed for two more, and threw it varial on the way back in. Christian was still amateur but warming up for his runs with back-to-back-to-back six-foot backsides. Any two of Lester Kasai's consecutive airs over Whittier's keyhole (backside or frontside) added up to sixteen feet. Neil Blender won the amateur one year with a straight-arm invert stalled so long that Glen E. Friedman had time to scramble over from the other side of the pool and get the photo (full page) for *Action Now*'s last issue. Billy Ruff would rock 'n' roll boardslide one-third of Del Mar's coping and reenter fakie. Duane actually hung up his front truck on a big backside reentry at Whittier and made it. The winner's check at these events: 500 bucks.

*Action Now* magazine was actually ahead of its time, using skateboarding to carry coverage of other dynamic sports like jet skiing, and horseback riding—just like the X/Gravity Games are doing now. *Thrasher Magazine* came out in 1981 with attitude and a mission statement that said, "by skaters, for skaters, and all about skateboarding." Skateboarders were out there and *Thrasher* knew they

**Top:** Afterschool catamaran comeraderie in San Mateo, CA, 1976.

**Center:** Mark Conohan barrels into a woodsy ramp somewhere in the Northwest corridor. On big backyard vert, the backside roll-in was mandatory if you wanted to session with the boys.

**Bottom:** Underneath the Eiffel Tower in Paris, the duck ponds at Trocadero have welcomed skaters from the world over.

would be there. Even if there was only one, it was reason enough to have a dedicated mag. Almost immediately, the proliferation of skate 'zines confirmed that skaters were out there, they had just gone underground. Building skate ramps was another way skaters took skateboarding back into their own hands. Looking for new skate terrain was always an adventure, one that skateparks almost eliminated. The adventure of a spot search with your friends and traveling and meeting skaters at their spots was a reason to skate in itself. Trading styles and stories, cranking tunes and staying on the move—even if you searched all day without skating anything, it was a blast. Skate culture was rising in the early 1980s and it didn't take long for skateboarders to discover and exploit the best and most obvious terrain that was right under their boards the whole time— the street.

Street skating was nothing new to the Dogtowners and the urchins who had always seen the potential in L.A. schoolyards, parking garages, and driveway runs. Only now there were a whole bunch of new ideas to try, and the terrain was unlimited and free with no rules except for the occasional cop chase. Cut to Skate City, Whittier's parking lot, and there was Lance Mountain, John Lucero, Neil Blender, and Richard Armijo sessioning a single parking block for hours on end. They would bring vert moves from the park to try in the street and street moves back into the park; that is, if they were allowed in the park. A lot of skaters were getting banned from skateboard parks, and who needed them? Rollerskating and BMX were happening again! Freestyle nerds like Steve Rocco and later Rodney Mullen were fooling around doing inverts off of flat ground, adding varials and finger flips just for fun. Where freestyle-met-vert-met-street in the early 1980s is when skateboarding took off again.

Parks began to close and doze even as Colton, CA cut the ribbon on a perfect new clamshell pool; the snake run there was the best ever but nobody showed up to ride it. A young Mike Smith won a contest in the Colton Clam, beating his idol Duane. Lance Mountain won the amateur division that day, serving notice for a whole new crew to emerge. The Gold Cup turned into the Rusty Harris Series turned into the National Skateboard Association, and vert skating still thrived with a generation of park-bred rippers. But even while the parks were there, as soon as board sales dropped off, the skate companies went into shock and didn't know what to do. When the parks were gone,

*Thrasher* magazine infused much-needed energy by throwing contests in the street and on skaters' backyard ramps. Mainly to create coverage for the mag, the first San Francisco Streetstyle, Joe's Ramp Jam, St. Pete Jam, Midwest Melee, Capitola Classic (street), and Savannah Slamma (arena-style) not only brought it to the skaters, but created a lot of new ones who realized that kicking a board around on the curb in front of 7-11 was OK.

Street pros and Vision Street Wear appeared almost simultaneously, as the skate companies that survived began to chip in. Powell Peralta, Santa Cruz, Vans, Gordon & Smith, Independent, Variflex, Sims, Walker, Gullwing, Madrid, Tracker—all were hanging on and hung in to see these efforts starting to pay off. Pro events began to hit every corner of the skating world—Clown Ramp, Dallas; Mt. Trashmore, Virginia Beach, Virginia; Mobile, Alabama; Sacramento, California; Chicago; Louisville—and skateboarding was on a roll. In fact, in 1986, skateboarding was so huge and worldwide that there was only one thing left to do: Press the reset button again. After Jeff Phillips won the NSA Holiday Havoc, playing to 5,000 screaming fans in the Anaheim Arena, skateboarding began to slide off into darker corners once again. Although many classic sessions and contests went down and the battles between Hawk and Hosoi were worth the price of admission alone, a purging was in order.

As the late 1980s blended into the early 1990s, street skating began to really take hold of the "what's happening" end of things. Vert was dying; there weren't enough kids interested nor enough places that had vert ramps to learn on. Street skating was everywhere and everybody could take part. The earlier simple street styles (jump ramp tricks, wall rides, slappies, tail stalls, etc.) had given way to much more technical skating, with more power and smoothness as the months went by. People like Matt Hensley, Jason Lee, Mike Vallely, Ed Templeton, Guy Mariano, and Brian Lotti were making the transition to cleaner technical skating; flip tricks were leaving ground level, curb tricks were becoming block tricks, block tricks were becoming rail tricks, boardslides became noseslides, one-footed ollies were kicked, ollie grabs were more tweaked. It was during this time of the early 1990s that a lot of the framework of modern street skating came to exist. Board shapes streamlined, wheels slimmed down, trucks got lighter, board rails faded out. The description of what made a "good skater" was starting to split between the tricks you could do versus

A streetplant session sprouts alongside Mt. Trashmore in Virginia Beach, VA, 1986.

Curb your dogs. Danny Sargent skated all terrains well but owned the double-sided, red Safeway curb off Market Street in San Francisco, where he worked out often to an appreciative local audience.

the style that you had, with only a select few able to straddle the fence between the two categories. Videos were becoming more and more important as the speed of street skating progressed. Videos such as H-Street's *Hokus Pokus*, Planet Earth's *Now 'n' Later*, and the infamous *Video Days* from Blind are excellent examples of what was coming to be.

A number of people began to push technical skateboarding to the limits a few years into the 1990s. Names like Mike Carroll, Henry Sanchez, Rick Howard, and Jovontae Turner became synonymous with whatever was the newest in tech; noseslide crooked grinds, bigspin kickflips, nollie flips, the unfortunate pressure flip period, backside tailslide shove-its; whatever was cool. New tricks were coming out at an explosive rate, and if you couldn't keep up, you couldn't be down. There was a seemingly endless bag of tricks to be mastered, and many of the old standards were being looked down upon. *Thrasher* once said that "the pressure flip is rapidly replacing the kickflip." Thank God that didn't happen. Happily, the tech explosion began to simmer down, and only the most useful, powerful, and stylish tricks stuck around (while the double flips, pressure flips, late flips, and extended curb dances went the way of the dodo).

While all of the tech mayhem was bubbling over, there were a handful of gnarly skaters still hungry to go big. Sean Sheffey, Pat Duffy, John Cardiel, Wade Speyer, Salman Agah, and others were still out conquering the biggest gaps, the longest rails, and the toughest power tricks. By the time 1994 appeared, these two categories were starting to merge. Guys like Jamie Thomas, Eric Koston, Chad Muska, Keith Hufnagel, Geoff Rowley, Chris Senn, Kris Markovich, and a growing list of others were taking flip tricks further and faster, down more steps and longer rails, and with more style and intensity. There were some skaters and teams who leaned towards one side or the other of the tech vs. clean-style division (Menace/All City/City Stars had the tech, for example, while the Stereo team simply oozed

with pure-style skaters), but all in all, skating was coming back to the point where you could do whatever you wanted, and it was cool as long as you did it well. This ideal reached a saturation point in the mid 1990s, as surprise returns of wallrides, no-complys, bonelesses, and other quirky and seemingly forgotten tricks made a big comeback. Everybody was having a lot of fun at this point, but progression was slowing down, and eventually skaters started demanding new tricks and faces. The *Mouse* video appeared and redefined technical skating for the mid-to-late 1990s, The Muska phenomenon was in full swing, handrails were practically all anybody wanted to skate, and a load of new faces began to appear from all over the world. Vert came back into "acceptance," and names like Bob Burnquist, Tas Pappas, Colin McKay, Andy MacDonald, Bucky Lasek, Tony Hawk, Rune Glifberg, Mike Frazier, and Danny Way made their way into the spotlight (some for the second or third time).

Skating in the late 1990s remained somewhat steady. The major change in skateboarding since then has been the sudden and massive media coverage and resurgence of skatepark construction. Entities like ESPN, MTV, Nike, the Gravity Games, and many more major sponsors began pumping money into skateboarding contests and parks, claiming that they were supporters. It is no longer uncommon to see a contest on television or an under-construction park in a small town. While these may seem like good things at the beginning, the industry has seen these things before, and the idea that the skateboard industry is heading for a crash in the near future has been discussed frequently in recent days. Will skateboarding head back to the parks? Back underground? In some entirely new direction? Whatever happens, we have new tricks, new people, new ideas, and the future of skateboarding in general to look forward to, and if you are truly down, you will help make it.

—T-ed
(*Compiled with props to Don Redondo, John Smythe, the Skipper, and Mark Whiteley.*)

Neil Blender was perfectly happy
sessioning a parking block all day
with a volley of street tricks; some,
like this no-comply over an
Alhambra Safeway stone, he
invented on the spot, named at
whim, and took to vert with mind-
blowing result.

In November 1980, the crew at High Speed Productions, Inc. printed the first issue of *Thrasher* magazine in San Francisco and started off on a journey into the dense jungle of the magazine publishing world, known for dangerous pitfalls and sinkholes. With enough capital to publish six monthly tabloid-size issues, with or without ad sales, the boys knew it would be a long hard road, with low pay and long hours.

Although the business of skateboarding had dropped off considerably by the end of the 1970s with skateshops and skateparks closing their doors as fast as they had opened them, there was still a healthy, underground contingency of hardcore skaters out there. *Thrasher* didn't orient its coverage toward manufacturers, shopkeepers or parents. Instead, we went for the gut—the kid on the street, the crew skating in your empty swimming pool. That's where skateboarding was in 1980 and we were in on the low end. If there was one skateboarder left out there, then *Thrasher* was for them.

For more than twenty years we've been accepted by this very fickle, very skeptical, very image- and peer-conscious audience that no other magazine has been able to reach on such a large scale. *Thrasher* is theirs. It is by and for them. We incorporate reader writing, art, and photography whenever possible, and our staff consists primarily of young adults who grew up with the mag or acquired their own reputation in the skate world before coming to work here.

Whether it be music, tricks, trends or culture, skateboarders, as a breed, stand fast against a sea of mediocrity. *Thrasher* is, was, and always will be about pushing the edge. This magazine is the longest running, non sell-out Bible of skateboarding simply because it is the unadulterated voice of the streets. In your face, in your backyard, or in the Smithsonian Institute, twenty years of *Thrasher* has changed the world forever.

First issue, *Thrasher Magazine*, January 1981. Skate scene—dead; Cover drawing by KT; printed on rag newsprint; feedback—"black ink rubbed off all over my girlfriends white skirt."

JANUARY 1981 $1.00

# THRASHER

## SKATEBOARD MAGAZINE ™

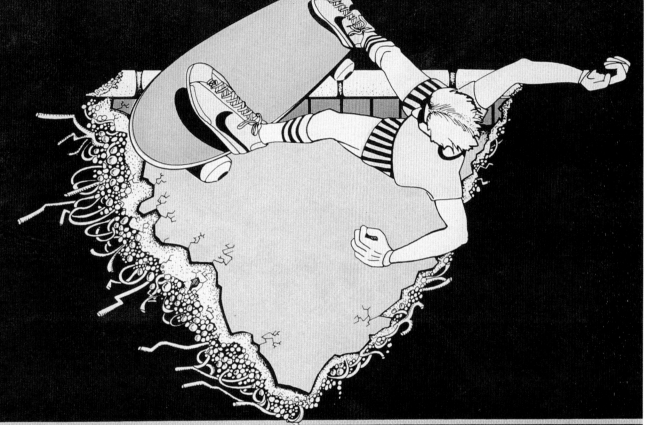

**IN THE STREET TODAY**

**DOWNHILL SKATEBOARD RACING**

**GOLD CUP FINAL**

Northwest skaters take trowel in hand to improve their lot. Abandoned digs in Seattle were patterned after the Burnside Project in Portland.

## MY FIRST TIME
*By Jake Phelps, January 1996*

It was a warm Spring afternoon in April 1975 when my life was changed forever. I started skateboarding. It happened innocently enough. Skateboarding was all the rage and I wanted to be hip, so naturally I was down. The first two years were lost in a world of grass rides, scabs, loose ball-bearing wheels, tic-tacs, friends, dirty clothes and worn-out shoes. Then, just as fast as everyone started, everyone quit. I can still hear their voices as they asked me, "You still skate?" I just shook my head and pushed away. They never got it. That was the dawn of the reality that most people never really do get it, they just go through the motions for acceptance, because going against the grain is too much work. Skateboarding transformed me from a sedated slug into an action addict. Always on the prowl for some new kind of kick, I found it looking in backyards for pools, stealing wood to build shitty half-pipes ten feet tall, bombing monster hills, burning down kids' ramps who wouldn't let us ride, getting chased by the pigs and basically telling all who crossed my path to get out of it. At fifteen, I was down for life. I spent the next ten years punishing my body to the physical extreme: broken bones, being hit by cars, punctures, hippers, swellbows, shinners, ankle folds—I was pushing limits in all aspects of life for that was how I wanted to die.

In 1989, I got a job at High Speed in the shipping department. It was the first nine-to-five job I ever had. I was happy to find employment at a place that understood what my life was all about, where you could express your opinion and not fear the ramifications. By always speaking my mind and calling bunk on what I thought was weak, I was asked to work in the editorial department, and in 1992, I assumed the role of the leader.

Skateboarding is my life. I don't have a car so you may see me on a rainy night—out of the corner of your eye, cruising down the sidewalk on my roadkill special—for I have miles to go before I sleep.

Keith Morris of the Circle Jerks leads a cheer.

Skateboarding . . . it's not for everybody, but you're welcome to try. Luge loser Alain O'Brocklin went for a near-death experience when he stuffed his rail into a Ford Pinto on Clipper Street in San Francisco. The impact actually pushed the car up on the sidewalk.

# HOW TO COPE WITH UNSTOKED PARENTS
*By Bonnie Blouin*

Every month we receive dozens of letters from kids asking how to cope with parents who are less than obliging to their skating needs. Some kids are heckled incessantly while others jones to skate and are simply not allowed because, as one skater reiterated, "Honey, it's too dangerous."

Lack of parental support, in my opinion, is a far worse crime than any restrictive bounds placed on skaters by cops, neighbors, etc. The real sorrow of this never ending saga is the amount of actual talent that is clipped and expunged by parents who refuse to acknowledge that skating is anything more than "a phase" or an annoying activity. Parents' blatant refusal to recognize the potential their son or daughter displays, combined with their inability to understand the amount of skill and expertise skateboarding requires, is an unfortunate hindrance to the progress of skateboarding.

## MOM'S PERSPECTIVE

Mothers are usually the main "stick in the mud" in a skater's household. This is likely due to the fact that when Mom was a teenager, skateboarding was a sprout, growing its first roots. Now, with her adult status and infinite wisdom, the thought of rolling down the street, much less Smith grinding a handrail, is unfathomable. Since Mom never saw much skateboarding in her younger, more flexible years, she may have a difficult time realizing that all your frontside flipping, crooked grinding, switch ollie feats are anything more than shin-bashing, knee-jarring, bone-breaking antics.

In other words, when Mom peers through the kitchen window to see you skating, she's not going to think, "Johnny's doing tre flips much better today," because her comprehension of any trick is probably nonexistent. My own mother, who witnessed daily shredding in her own backyard for years, still cannot distinguish between frontside and backside. So, all your mom actually sees from a nonskater's eyeball view is you flailing about on four wheels. Tack on the "momism" factor and you are, in her eyes, narrowly escaping death.

## DAD'S PERSPECTIVE

Dad is usually a bit more lax as he was probably accustomed to the bumps and bruises of physical sports as a youngster. Again, though, since skating was probably not one of his adolescent activities, Dad's eyeball view is much like Mom's, although his terms of exacerbation come from a source other than "You're going to kill yourself."

Dads tend to have this scary notion that the ONLY sports are football, basketball, and baseball, or whatever sport he himself may have excelled in as a teenager. Therefore, while he may tolerate the fact that you skate, he will usually come up with a statement like, "You won't get a scholarship riding a skateboard," or "I don't know why you ever quit soccer to ride that thing." You know the deal; it's always on the tip of his tongue.

## DOUBLE TROUBLE

If you think you have it tough now, put your feet in some female Vans. The fact that this is [2001] hardly deters Mom and Dad from thinking skateboarding is a male sport that will only bring degradation to their young daughter.

Though we may appear a tad hoidenish as we romp around with a slew of young men, we're just Americans taking part in a healthy all-American sport. So our bruised shins aren't very ladylike and our shirts resemble paper bags with oranges stuffed inside. There are worse things, like drugs, vandalism, and shoplifting.

You'd think Mom and Dad would be pleased that we're athletes rather than overweight cellulotic blobs with no future. Besides, knitting and quilting just aren't for everyone.

## DEALING WITH MOM AND DAD

Communicating with your parents is the only way to alleviate this tension and avoid further confrontation. If you've ever noticed, Mom and Dad will usually rag on you the most during stressful moments. For instance: when they arrive home from the office after spending an hour in traffic; when they're late for an appointment; or after they've unsuccessfully attempted to perform repairs on a household appliance better left to a pro.

Feel your way around these moments. Wait 'till your parents are more relaxed before you hand them your report card or ask them if you can go with Johnny to skate the new ramp. Most importantly, you need to pick a quiet, casual time to say, "Hey, we need to talk." Ask them specifically why they disapprove of your skating and listen to their views.

Naturally, they will mention things you disagree with, but keep your cool. After all, they are speaking from the "Mom and Dad eyeball" and it's up to you to enlighten them. Don't blow it by blurting out something drastic in defense of your stance. As soon as you start stomping your feet and yelling, "I don't care what you say" type stuff, you've lost the battle. They won't stand for that.

Approach them with confidence; speak clearly and with conviction. Make it understood, by your voice and your actions, that you are serious and you expect some truthful answers. Parents will often blow a sticky situation off with the "I'm your mother and I said no" type response. Don't let it get to that point. This usually means they are ticked off or stressed out. Drop the subject and wait until they are calm to bring it up again. If they never seem calm, you'll just have to harsh it out. You have a right to express your views.

Once you know what your parents' views are, whomp 'em with your own. Elaborate on their negative reasons and clear them up. If they mention that skateboarding is dangerous, explain the use of safety equipment and falling techniques (rolling, knee sliding, etc.). If they claim that it's too expensive, offer to earn money.

If your grades are suffering or your parents dislike your friends and the way you dress, you might be in for a rough ride. They tend to use those things against you. In this case, you will probably have to prove to them, by bringing up your grades, etc., that skating is not the downfall of your teenage years. It is up to you to provide positive counter responses to their negative reasons. This will leave them with nothing to argue about.

The next step is explaining to them what skating means to you and why. They don't know what it's like to tweak a stalefish over a hip. They don't know why it thrills you, day after day, to learn new moves and feel your board under your feet. You have to tell them.

Skating is more than just a sport; it's a way of life. Stick with it. You parents will get the idea sooner or later, so keep your chin up and skate with pride.

## GRAB THAT BOARD
*Editorial by Kevin Thatcher, January 1981*

How many times have you heard someone say, "Skateboards—yeah, I remember we used to take our sister's rollerskates and mount the wheels on a two by four." Or, today's favorite, "Are you guys involved in the X Games at all?" The problem here is a lack of understanding of what skateboarding is all about. The average individual was never properly exposed to the unlimited possibilities of a platform with four wheels under it—a simple, basic mechanical device which serves as an energy efficient mode of transportation, a basis for a valid sporting activity, and as a vehicle for aggressive expression.

At the height of the commercial skatepark explosion in the late seventies, skaters were virtually swept off the streets and deposited in the parks. The action was radical but lacked the intensity of a knock-down, drag-out backyard pool session or a skate cruise down the boulevard with the crew. The fact is skateboarding can survive without skateparks, but the parks will never last without skaters, as a whole, to support them. Many times I have wired a new trick in the street only to find myself the next day at the park trying to perfect it on the vertical. Skateparks are fun. Streetskating is fun, and also visual. The whole world is out there, waiting to be entertained, but they want it delivered to their doorstep. So let's deliver!

THRASHER was born out of a need for intense and objective reporting on an activity that has established itself as a major pastime for many people and a rewarding experience for countless others. "Thrashing" is an attitude, a skate attitude. Thrashing is part of a lifestyle, a fast-paced feeling to fit this modern world. Thrashing is finding something and taking it to the ultimate limit—not dwelling on it, but using it to the fullest and moving on. Skateboarding has not yet reached its maximum potential, and who can say what the limits are. To find out—Grab that board! You don't have to be a super-talented professional skater. Grab that board if you're a novice having some fun on a Saturday afternoon.To the kid hanging out at the Stop'n'Shop with his gang—Grab that board! To the college student who needs a vehicle to get from dorm to class—Grab that board! And how about the dad who calls his kid crazed for riding a skateboard all the time—Grab that board! There are no rules saying that you have to go fast or skate vertical. Just being outside or in the skatepark practicing maneuvers (tricks) and balance is a lot of fun. Remember, there is tons of asphalt and concrete being poured every day, so—Grab that Board!

These guys don't skate.

Skaters on patrol pause during Desert Storm, Kuwait.

Founding *Thrasher* editor "KT," casual cut back, Uvis Dam, 1976

Michael Henry, Los Altos Pool, 1976

"The Rubberman," Dr. Rick Blackhart, fakie 360 edge-out, Upland Hester Series, 1978

Andy Croft, wailing wall, Daly City, CA, 1975

Original Skate Mechanic, Del 13

Layout master, Mofo, Notre Dame, Paris

the future

xas ringleader, Jeff "Newtron" Newton, pogo sticking

Kieth Stephenson, aka "Billy Runaway," tucks pipe to pipe

OG city boy and photo pro, Bryce Kanights, burls off his kicker ramp in GG Park, San Francisco

Pierre and skate pup

*Thrasher* editor Jake Phelps, precarious nollie-oop at Strat's Ramp.

Mr. V brings the bank and a first place check to Caballero at Joe Lope's Backyard Ramp Jam Barbeque and Bake-off, 1984

# PHOTOGRAFFITI

PAGE 19    PHOTO A        100%

## The Low Road

### $400 Million on Wheels

*Newsweek 11/14/77*

Skateboard World, outside Los Angeles, is a forbidding-looking place, a 3½-acre, concrete moonscape of bone-scorching dimes and valleys, bowls and channels. Day after day, especially during the post-supper rush, it is packed with "carvers" and "boinkers" who pay $2 for

It's a business that's aimed at the very young. The average skateboarder in southern California is only 14, according to one survey, and at Skateboard World, no one over 40 has ever been seen on a board. Yet each of those average skateboarders owns more than $100 worth of

teboard enthusiasts found a new, arching challterstate 805 in San Diego. The graceful curves of

the huge cement supports for the highway overpass provided a sport for the youngsters to roll on in relative quiet and safety.

## Free as a board

Speedracing, slaloming, headstands, pirouettes— that's what skateboarders are into.

**Up the wall:** The object is to go as high as you can (this embankment, at a skateboard competition in Asbury Park, N. J., is 15 feet), then turn without falling and zoom down.

Kent Senatore, shallow end involvement at the Ranch.

### Boarders

Continued from Page 40

But Gregg has recently taken to wearing shoes. "My toe was beginning to feel the pain. My feet just couldn't take it anymore."

"The boom's leveling off out here, but only because California's now saturated. It's still mushrooming everywhere else," reports Warren Bolster, editor of SkateBoarder, a southern California magazine with a press run of 200,000

130 p    ...including 50 pages of advertise-
ments.    ...to turn away

now...

en Sporting Goods      pic
...et in New York f     St. Broad
f sales began to     laso
selling 50 s     at ABC Christma
ome curv     y Page 100 Skateboards
ards     ed Jimmy     omers purchasing
time     suit up     places    say's Howard
autho     in cras    ber    this time

Getting down to it: At Conservatory Lake in Central Park, a Manhattan skateboard hangout.

comes off a ramp at a skateboard meet in Uniondale, N. Y. Others ...ards by working up speed, rotating their bodies and jumping.

**Doubles:** Like many California skateboarders, these two, doing the "Side Bird," are also surfers.

Eye contact with Arthur Lake.

Every night fever.

WYNN MILLER

WORLD PROFESSIONAL SKATEBOARD CHAMPIONSH

Tony Alva blew minds when he broke the barrel jumping record for the second straight year.

# gallery

## Tall Tale

Lembert Dome in Tuolomne Meadows is one mountain skateboard enthusiast Dave Liston didn't skate down. But it makes a great story, as told by photographer Fred Clements of Manhattan Beach.

### COUNTY ENACTS BAN
## State Panel Curbs Motor Skateboard

The same urge that drives youngsters from toy pistol to BB gun to rifle, now has kids on motorized skateboards.

No longer is it simply leg power that propels the slender boards, but a 1.2-horsepower engine that can push them at 20

with human-powered skateboards.

The motorized variety is beginning to proliferate, Oliver said, and Hayden's bill would prevent accidents.

Technically, motorized skateboard operators are subject to

*Tues., July 20, 1976*

Young skateboard buffs roared down a sidewalk below the Cliff House

San Jose Mercury Monday, September 19, 1977

# Skateboard-park developers eye valley's big potential

By GARY SWAN
Staff Writer

Remember the last time a skateboarder almost ran you off the sidewalk with your bag of groceries?

How about the last time you had to jam on your brakes as a skateboarder and its youthful rider came scooting off a driveway?

Haven't you sometimes wished there was a place you could have nicely told them to go?

There soon will be several such places in the San Jose area as entrepreneurs race to beat each other, and perhaps the clock, into the skateboard park field.

In the last year, 40 skateboard parks have sprung up around the country, mainly in Florida and Southern California. In Los Angeles alone, 20 parks are reportedly doing a booming business.

Locally, plans are in varying stages for skateboard parks on Miramonte Avenue near El Camino Real in Mountain View, on South Bascom Avenue in Campbell; and on the south side of Stevens Creek Boulevard between Hwy. 280 and San Tomas Expressway.

State and local governments have begun to come down hard on skateboarders who use the public way. There's a new California law prohibiting use of motorized skateboards on ...

All skateboard parks must require that participants wear safety gear — helmets, knee pads and elbow pads — to conform to insurance requirements.

## The Skateboard Boom Rolls On

### Friends Jaw At Pit Stops

By Michael Grieg

A skateboard-scarred veteran of 15 was comparing wounds and wheels yesterday with other enthusiasts of the big roller revival.

"This is my pride and joy," Burt Witaschek told those who had assembled at Skateboard City, a pit stop shop in the Sunset district that's one of the new phenomena of the booming sport.

He wasn't referring to his $55 Banzai aluminum board with urethane wheels and sealed bearings, capable of whizzing down city hills at 35 miles an hour or more. He

### Zooming Through an Aqueduct
## Where the Skateboards Flow

Phoenix

The giant Central Arizona Project has become something of a headache for some government officials, Indians, farmers and environmentalists, but it's a dream come true to a generation growing up on skateboards.

The $1.7 billion project to carry Colorado river water to central Arizona was cut early this year from the federal budget by President Carter. The project has been restored, however, and work has resumed.

While adults debate whether it really is needed or will supply enough water when ...

deputies, officials of the U.S. Bureau of Reclamation and the Ameron Corp., manufacturer of the pipes, skateboard enthusiasts have been sneaking into the pipes near Lake Pleasant every weekend.

"We've put up no-trespassing signs. Deputies are out there checking and citing kids all the time. We have five-to-ten-foot barricades at the ends of the pipes, but they still come," said Robert Sevitz, Ameron project manager.

Insurance problems increased, Sevitz said, after an article appeared in Skate Boarder magazine showing the desert discovery with the "pros" doing fakies and kickturns and soaring 11 feet up the big pipes.

Largest in the world, the pipes measure 21 feet in diame-

Skateboarders maneuvered through a section of 'the best skateboard park in the world'

ter inside, are 22 feet long and weigh 225 tons. The ones at the Lake Pleasant site will provide a 5000-foot-long syphon ... Agua Fria, New and Salt ...

months in jail and a $300 fine, the lure of the largest pipe in the world to a dedicated skate-

"I think the skateboarders first discovered the pipes at a factory near San Clemente, California. Sevitz said, plant manager allowed them to try them out and that whetted their appetites.

Although the maximum penalty for trespassing is ...

Since then, official permission has been denied movemakers to use the pipes, he said, but ...

Burt Witaschek, Greg Praeger and Brad Iwafuchi talked shop

from his allowance and odd jobs

Brad Iwafuchi, 15, was describing some of the best areas in the city for skateboarding.

"I like the Cliff House hill, out near Hoover Junior High, the Junior Museum over ... street way... I've gotten to speed to 35 miles an hour. Let me tell you you do a lot of wobbling at ... speed."

He and the others said they would like to see a skateboard in the city, similar to ones in ... City and elsewhere.

"It could have a banked course or two to suit those at different levels of skill," one skateboarder said. "Old Playland-at-the-Beach, now gone, would be a good spot for it."

Of course, a skateboard ...

LEE COLE
He said it's here to stay

Jay's radicalization of the Dog Bowl.

## MAY
# 22ND
9 am - 6 pm
# 23RD
9 am - 6 pm

NORTHERN CALIFORNIA
PRO - AM
SKATEBOARD CHAMPIONSHIP
Co-Sponsored By KFRC•610  At The
# COW PALACE

$2.00
UNDER 12 YEARS

$2.50
ADULTS

PROFESSIONAL AND AMATEUR COMPETITION
WORLD RECORD ATTEMPTS • 360° • HIGH JUMP
GIANT SLALOM RAMP • DOWNHILL SPEED • POOL SKATEBOARDING
SAFETY CLINICS • USE AND CARE CLINIC • DEMONSTRATIONS
• FILMS • SNEAK PREVIEW "THAT MAGIC FEELING" • FILMS
PRODUCT EXHIBIT BOOTHS
GO FOR IT!

# THE SKATERS

Everyday unknown, ripper, ruler, trog, and trilobyte.
Slashdog, tech gnar, freshie, and freak. Would-be,
wannabe, will be, and wierdo. Skateboarding brings the
rebels, punkers, outlaws, individualists, and daredevils
together on common ground. When a spot turns up and the
session goes down, you never know who will show up.
Skateboarding brings them out of their holes, but without
skaters . . . we got nothing.

Neil Blender, who routinely made tricks
that nobody has attempted since, creeps
past the edge of Del Mar Skatepark's
fabled hole.

Peter Smolik is a modern pro skateboarder having a good time.

Christian Hosoi, glamour boy of the eighties

Jay Adams and another young ripper from Venice area, George Watanabe, diggin' the scene

Young Tony Hawk shows he has the edge.

Beastie Boys share some gear with friends and crew backstage.

Jovontae Turner stylin' chopped Van's and frayed baggies, setting the style for a new street crew to follow.

**Above:** Bucky Lasek gettin' evil during lean times on the vert circuit.
**Right:** Brothers of different mothers. Texas pride: Todd Prince, Jeff Phillips, Ken Fillion, and John Gibson—all for one, care for none, just havin' fun.

The first time you step on a skateboard pretty much determines whether one is regular foot (left forward) or goofy (right forward). After that it's all a matter of style, interpretation, skill, and balls. And you can bet your buds are going to be critiquing your technique all the way. Push mongo-foot or lead with your fists and take it on the chin. Six gun, lead-foot, cringer, hinger, sasquatch, stinkbug, shit-footer, stomper, natural, styli, or squidly—hey, if you're at least skating—who cares?

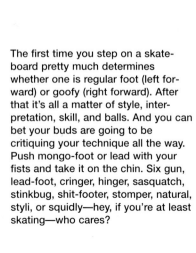

Sidewalk surfin' revisited. Scott Oster sets his line and his Air 1's with a high-speed four-wheel drift across the lip of "Charlene's," another secret spot in the hills above skate mecca Los Angeles.

Jake Phelps lays it down at HP Ramp, San Francisco.

Jeff Phillips shows a lot of pop for a big guy and a stylish tuck through a tight square corner.

Nobody looked like Craig Johnson and few will ever skate like him. Break time on the banks at a public skatepark outside Melbourne.

Alan "Ollie" Gelfand may have brought the no-handed air to the front, but he could grab 'em with the best at Surf Expo in Orlando, Florida.

Unsafe at any speed. Simple skate technology has inspired countless widgets and contraptions, none as good as a wood plank pivoting over four urethane wheels.

Gonz's high ollie grab over Lance Mountain's slash grind, during this night-time mini frenzy near Melbourne, OZ, was neither planned nor accidental, as Hosoi will attest.

ark "Gator" Rogowski had the skills to perform the frontside Rocket Air in
ny Hawk's face at Torquay Ramp Riot, Australia.

Wade Speyer in thrift store attire is the
king of pop for a hand-on ollie 180 down
city streets.

You don't hang up, ever," says Mark
Gonzales about the roto board he cooked
up one afternoon.

There's a fringe element surrounding
the skateboard scene that's always
good for a laugh and even the occasional sick trick. They may be hangers
or lurkers, used-to-skates or everyday
nightmares, but just give 'em an elbow to the rib and a few encouraging
words and watch them go off.

"There are those who have fallen, and those who will
fall." Scotty B looks it right in the eye during an unfortunate dirtboarding accident, Lee Vining, CA, 1993.

FREAK SHOW

Dropping in. Dave Hackett holds the line for a special delivery in NYC, 1987.

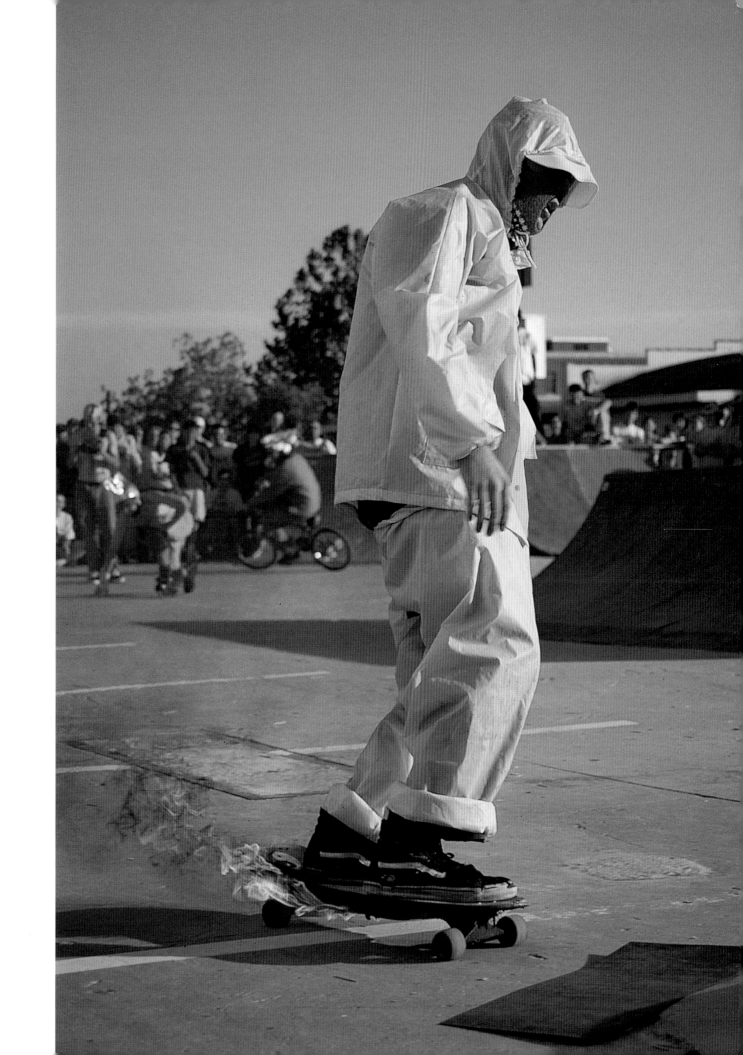

Christian Hosoi and
Pat Nogho getting rave
reviews in Japan.

Skaters come and go, especially
some who turn pro. After you've
waded through all the flash-in-the-
pan, one-trick wonders and would-be
number ones, the free product, board
royalties, and shoe deals—there are a
handful of skateboarders whose
names are always mentioned as legend. Over the years, there have been
those whose skating and manner
stand out above the rest. They turn
up heat at any session and raise the
bar at any contest they choose to
enter. Skaters who can win at will and
make it or break it on command,
leaving jaws dropped and hearts
stopped, deserve everything they get
out of skating because they've given
so much more.

# TONY ALVA

### TONY ALVA

Whenever skaters who've been any-where get together to talk about skateboarding, there's one name that makes it into the conversation. Tony Alva is known from the jungles of Hollywood to the tip of South America. New skaters come and go but there is only one TA. He's the original aggressive skater, with an unmistakable style—on and off the board. Whether liked or not, Tony Alva has been one of the most influential forces in skateboarding.

## MARK GONZALES

In a hot, dirty parking lot at the first Sacto streetstyle contest in 1985, a kid named Mark Gonzales introduced his own brand of skating to the world. Over the next fifteen years he went from being a little scrub to the king of modern-day street skating. Gonz lives in a world that few could ever comprehend. A Sharpie, an old Sims Taperkick, Baby Cujo, a telephone, and a fax machine are all he needs to get by.

MARK GONZALES

JAY ADAMS
The central element—the only one of any importance—is that Adams remains one of the great enigmas in the world of skateboarding. A prime innovator throughout the seventies and much sought after as a commercial entity, Jay seemingly made every effort to avoid the "successful life." During that fat period, when countless less talented sorts made big bucks off skating, Adams meticulously sought only undiluted, uncensored, and uncomplicated thrills. Much to the promoter's chagrin, Jay would regularly choose to disappear off into the tropics rather than keep in line for the movie gigs, mag covers, and assorted other trappings of fame and fortune.
—Lowboy, August 1982

JAY ADAMS

**TONY HAWK**

**TONY HAWK**
If one person has dominated the sport, it's Tony Hawk. Spit upon by Duane as a child, even as he performed Miller Flips at the scumline of Whittier Skatepark's keyhole pool, Hawk came to manhood by redefining the art of vertical skateboarding. His unbelievable legacy of trick development includes: ollie 540s, 720s, kickflip 540s, and the 900. Hawk will live forever as the supreme technician and as an ambassador of modern skateboarding's acceptance of it during its prime time.

**CHRISTIAN RASHA HOSOI**
Legend in skateboard circles, Christian Hosoi's status has busted far beyond the boundaries of just those in the know. The poster boy for skate style throughout the eighties; consistent top three contender at every major vert, street, or mini-ramp contest; the Hosoi air show was consistently over eight feet—back to back as he traveled the world spreading a positive vibe about skateboarding. After every event, contest, or demo—long after everyone was already out—Christian was there, signing autographs, talking to skaters; Christ was always respectful to moms, dads, and fans alike. Christian Hosoi could skate any terrain and charged every skate situation with a precision and flair that said "superstar" and backed it up with the baddest skating you'd ever seen. In the history of the sport, no name is more synonymous with power, style, and finesse than Holmes.

# CHRISTIAN HOSOI

**STEVE CABALLERO**

Caballero showed up at Campbell Skatepark sheathed in plastic and padding from fingertip to toe cap and proceeded to light a fire that burns to this day. Highlights include: frontsides across the gorge-like Winchester Pool channel, Caballerials, and more signature moves than any other skater. Caballero won professional skateboard contests in the 1970s, 1980s, and 1990s, and is now pacing himself into his fourth decade of skateboarding. He is a certified Bones Brigadeer general, musician, producer, husband, and daddy, not in any particular order, though hundreds of thousands of his fans know him simply as one of skateboarding's all-time bests.

STEVE CABALLERO

## DUANE PETERS

Stabbed, beaten, broken, and bloodied, Duane Peters has definitely paid his dues. He's invented more tricks than he can remember and done things few will ever forget. To this day, his style is unapologetically old school, and you can bet he doesn't give two O'Henry's what anyone thinks.

DUANE PETERS

## Eric Koston's Number Ones

#1 Trick: Rolling away.
#1 Vegetable: Spinach.
#1 Skater from the Seventies: Eddie Elguera.
#1 Book: I don't read.
#1 Appliance: TV.
#1 Video Part: Mark Gonzales, *Video Days*.
#1 Companion Animal: Dog.
#1 Relative: Mom.
#1 Synonym for "Rad": "Fuckin' rad."
#1 Pool Move: Backside one-footed carve grind.
#1 Excuse: It's too dark.
#1 Religion: Buddhism.
#1 Contest Obstacle: Hotel.

#1 Hiding Place: Home.
#1 Sea Creature: Manatee.
#1 Piece of Furniture: Couch.
#1 Ridiculous Purchase: House.
#1 Meal While in Germany: Chinese food.
#1 Phone Call: Girlfriend.
#1 Reason to Quit: Someone telling you that they made you.
#1 Childhood Hero: Luke Skywalker.
#1 Annoyance: Traffic.
#1 Vacation Spot: Thailand.
#1 Pet Name: Billie.
#1 Plan for the Future: Retire.

ERIC KOSTON

## ERIC KOSTON

Eric Koston came to the scene during a period in the late eighties when skateboarding was flat and ripe for a change. Change came in the form of a next generation of super-talented, super-tech board pilots that made skate spots appear where none had existed before and turned tricks that had not been comprehended. Suddenly skaters were turning pro with a video clip and contests were out. So, Koston went out and schooled the best in every contest he entered *and* got it on video.

# OMAR HASSAN

## OMAR HASSAN

From Blockhead to Black Label, Omar led the early 1990s crossover legions by taking the best of vert and the budding technicality of street straight to the new era of minis. The protégé of Caballero, an all-around nice guy, and a winner of bowl and pool contests even to this day, Omar hasn't laid back after the guard switched over but has organized the change himself.

**EAN SHEFFEY**
katers today use the term "tech-
nar" to describe someone who has
e ability to go big and fast, all while
rowing down technical wizardry.
When the *Life* video came out in
992, an eighteen-year-old unknown,
ho would soon be recognized by the
orld as "Sheff," burned the screen
ith huge backside ollies over park-
g lot islands. If you see him coming
t you, get outta the way because big
heff doesn't care. If there's some
n, he's gonna have it.

**OB BURNQUIST**
fter winning the first pro contest he
ver entered by making everyone
tare and want to hide their eyes at
e same time, blazing Brazilian Bob
urnquist has quickly gone on to mark
ut a place in skateboard history that
 his alone. His mastery of all ter-
ains, and his ambidextrous innova-
on on vert, make it no wonder that
ob is Tony Hawk's favorite skater.

# BOB BURNQUIST

WADE SPEYER

# GEOFF ROWLEY

**GEOFF ROWLEY**

Geoff Rowley is everything I think a pro skater should be. He's a good friend and one of my favorite people to skate with. He's always pushing himself to the limit.
—Chad Muska

When I'm afraid to try something, I think that if it were Geoff, he wouldn't hesitate. He would just attack. His hunger is a constant fire under my ass.
—Jamie Thomas

**WADE SPEYER**

One of the first times I ever skated with Wade outside a demo/contest atmosphere was when he just started riding for Powell. Steve Sherman and I drove up to his house to shoot video and went to some of his spots with him. I remember one ledge that was on the side of a LONG driveway. It was one of those wide ledges that your trucks barely clear when you ride it (it was too rough to grind). You needed a pretty high ollie up to it, then a steady slide to the end—actually you had to come off before the end or you'd wind up in the plants. The middle part was probably six to eight feet off the ground. I tried it a couple of times but I couldn't make it through the middle without sketching out. You just never knew if your board was gonna stop and send you head first off the side. Wade made it first try: clean all the way through—only he had to do it frontside.
—Tony Hawk

# BOMBIN' HILLS

Layed out. Lee Danzie casually no-looks while careening down a mountain on what looks like an auto shop creeper you might use to slide under your car, but not at sixty miles an hour.

Tony Alva leads with his chin, dropping into a Beverly Hills bowl at top speed. Whatever the situation, whatever the terrain, Alva is game for skating and he will make his presence known.

Mainlining. Fred Smith speed carves a
roadside Roxbury ditch in Boston, MA.

SIDEWALK SURFIN'

An abandoned, bleached white motel pool on the shores of the Salton Sea is close to Heaven-on-earth for some skaters—mere mortals want nothing to do with it.

One of the most popular skate locales has been the drained swimming pool. Long after the kiddies with their life preservers and the yuppies with their pool-side parties have deserted their pools, some of these structures, now drained, have excellent curves and gradations and quickly become the perfect hangouts for skaters.

Jeff Phillips went on to become one of the world's best vert champions but his roots were skating Texas plaster with the crew.

unique backyard pool configuration in a swank golf-course community outside Honolulu does not go unnoticed, or unskated, by the local boys.

Still guilty during more innocent times. Empty pools were abundant on the West Coast during drought years in the seventies. Andy Croft test carves Los Altos pool before kooks ripped out the coping, sawed off the ladders, painted it orange, and got photos in the mag.

One of the great pool skaters, Ruben Orkin, grinds a perfect kidney keeper.

Outtake from June 1984 cover shoot. Mark "Gator" Rogowski hit this freshly drained, kinked-out backyard pool from every angle including this lapover into the shallows.

Attack with enough speed and snap, and something's got to give. David Hackett power ollies make-or-break style over the "death box."

ben Orkin performs the delicate alleyoop Rube-a-dupe, grinding backwards into the shallow end.

shallow end frontside grind, over the steps . . . doesn't get any tougher, but seasoned pool player Royce Nelson makes it look smooth.

Mark Jones takes a smooth line through the heel of an abandoned L-pool in the desert that is Southern California.

Christian Hosoi lays back hard on some cruel square coping during a morning shade pool hit in Phoenix.

Julien Stranger stands up to the burl that is C-pool in Cambridge, Massachusetts. Note the twelve-foot mark, kinked tranny, and Julien's line that started before the death star and carried him over the box.

Border patrol. If you can't locate this pool on the Mexi-Cali border after seeing the clues in this photo, then you don't skate . . . or don't care. It's probably been filled with dirt anyway, and the building in the background is the local police department. Just don't tell them we sent you.

Buena Vista pool near Santa Cruz has been skated off and on for more than thirty-five years. Al Losi skated Buena one day.

Feeling no pain. Barefoot, baked, and mud-caked in the Hawaiian sun, Kale Sandridge works any empty pool that crosses his path. Kale rips bowls so thoroughly sometimes even he doesn't know which direction his stance is going.

Government issue. Brian Brannon applies a hands-on approach to the unique beveled transition and spit gutter configuration of Bastrop pool at an abandoned army outpost in Texas.

The abundant square footage of the receiving pool at San Jose's Raging Waters slide park is scoured for a rare throw down.

Mike McGill and Tony Hawk perform side by side 540s on a shaky demo ramp before thousands of fans in downtown Sydney, Australia.

To have your own skatespot right in the backyard is an attainable dream that many saavy skaters have realized. Pop out of bed, put on the coffee, feed the cats, and strap on the pads and helmet. You built it, you skate it, you rule it. No other backyard "sport" has caused such a proliferation of crafted structures on such a scale as skateboarding. From building driveway quarter pipes to mega Chin-styled, multi-bowled, and spined monoliths, skateboarders continue to demonstrate the positive effects of mixing creativity with a little insanity.

RAMPS

Kasai High. Lester would go bio until he exploded but his third air was usually clocking in the ten-foot range like this one over the blue monster at Houston Skatepark.

A small backyard mini ramp cannot contain the thrust of Dave Chavez, so he just takes it to the stucco and off the side of the house.

Thanks Mike. Legendary sessions a
Mile High Ramp on Lake Tahoe's
north shore culminated in the Terro
contest and the infamous product
toss (which might have also includ-
ed a dead cat) turned warzone.

Christian Hosoi, tipped out frontside
body bone, on his ramp. Los
Angeles, CA

Wade's garage, Concord, CA, 1994

**Previous Spread:** Sunday picnic. A three-day demo on the Shake billboard half pipe inside the Formula 1 circuit in Adelaide, Australia, was a rather casual affair. Lee Ralph and Mark Gonzales are in there somewhere.

re you ready for some football? Well, no. Little fans dragged along to daddy's games remember the halfpipe on Monday night and the names of the inverted demo dogs who performed. Fifteen years later, ratings down—skateboarding up. Thanks ABC—you did rule.

One of the world's best in any skate-boarding arena, Phil Shao said that this ollie to top bar out of the "killer capsule" in Madrid, Spain, was the gnarliest thing he had done in a long time.

Good, Bad . . . Ugly. Except for Kona Skatepark in Jacksonville, Florida, none of more than two hundred commercial skateparks built in the United States in the late seventies survived the bulldozer. Does the same fate await the hundreds of public skate facilities being installed across the land today? Some are so poorly designed as to be dangerous.

Aproador bowls in Rio de Janiero straddle the peninsula between world-class beach real estate.

Weston Creek on the Australian skatepark trail offers up a myriad of finally radiused and crisp-lipped possibilities for Dan Drehobl to float over.

Young Tommy Guerrero knuckle drags an early grab over the hip of a sweet snake run at Victoria in Milpitas, CA.

Worldly perfect. Skateparks can be fun when they are prepared and served well done, no frills, by a competent staff. Livingston, Scotland boasts one of the first and foremost government-sponsored dishes and Livi's designs still hold Alan Petersen's air eighteen years after Caballero and the Bones Brigade cut the ribbon.

Fly by. Bob Burnquist ollie crosses the gap at
Guara Country Club, on the road to Rio from
São Paulo, Brazil.

ee Ralph is a big man to be
rinding the tight and deadly
4 pipe at Nunawading, out-
de Melbourne.

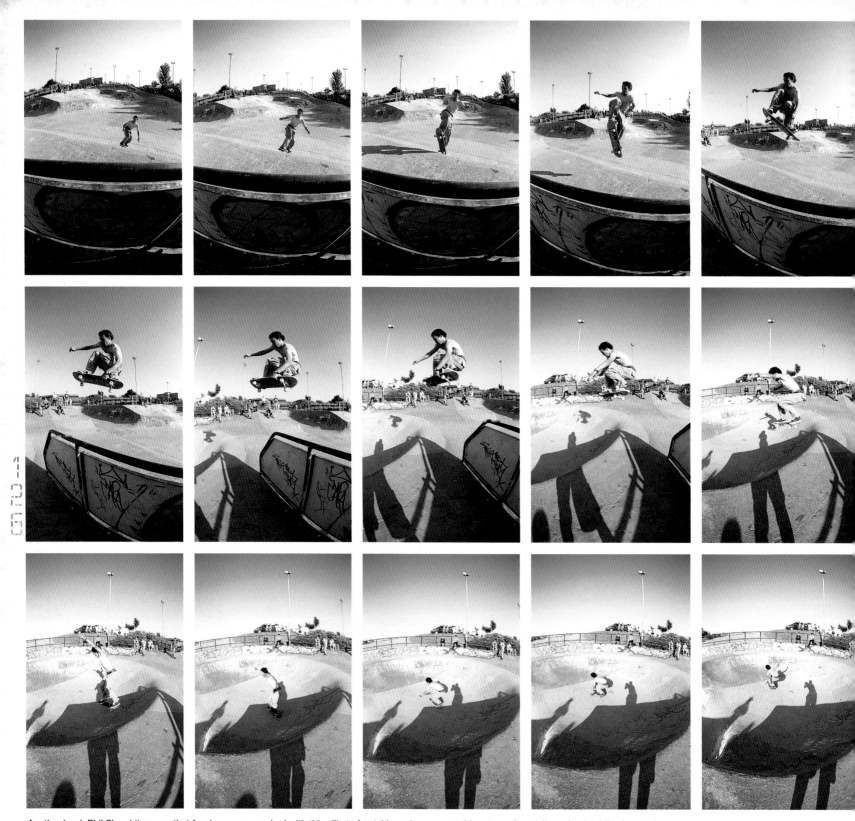

Another level. Phil Shao hit a zone that few have ever reached with this ollie to frontside grab over everything at another well-received public skatepark.

**This Page and Facing Page:** Mark Scott launches out and over a public park he designed and constructed in Lincoln City, Oregon. Some claim its crisp and fast contours to be the gnarliest yet.

Now living outside San Diego, world champ Bob Burnquist often returns to his homeland spots in South America to rework a line like this down time tail drop inbetween traffic jams.

# STREETS

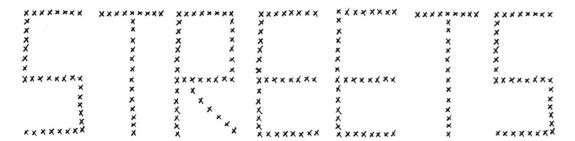

A curb is an obstacle until you grind across it. A wall is but a ledge until you drop off it. A cement bank is a useless slab of concrete until you shred it. A street is another downhill to be tucked. A multi-level garage is built for cars until a gang of skaters discovers it. You've got to give the btrreets fair due—rolling is way cooler than walking. Don't restrict your boundaries—skate architecture is everywhere—grind every edge. You've gotta find all the lines you can.

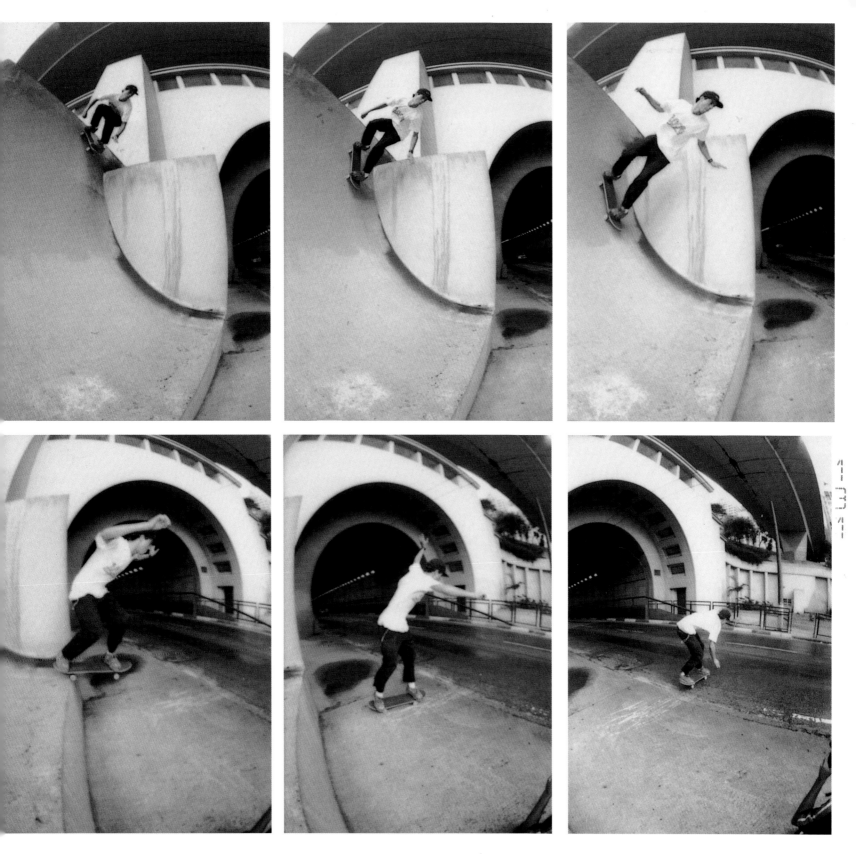

Cairo Foster may have moved the dumpster into his path down the sidewalk . . . skaters have been known to exhibit such behavior.

ll aboard. Matt Hensley had just graduated from the academy when he found this roller coaster rail in Mission Beach near San Diego, before
e became a real bona-fide pro street star.

Flashpoint. Jamie Thomas usually catches up to any reputation that preceeds him but stays pretty humble about routinely launching himself down thirty-five feet of landscaping for a living.

Most pros can stick the tre-flip on ugly inclines such as this one, but Rick Howard managed to reproduce this *Thrasher* cover outtake with a little yellow plastic banana board.

Hubba MC. Coming up together in San Francisco, Mike Carroll got to know Hubba Hideout's famous ledges pretty well, so this switch backside for Smith wasn't too much of a problem. The Hubba ledge has gone on to become a featured element of every new skatepark and contest design.

New school. When the street scene came to the front in the early nineties Jesse Martinez escaped from Venice and unleashed a furious assault on every plane. Here, "the Mess" shows several hundred locals at a schoolyard demo in Honolulu how to hit the bricks and make a wall walk heli-spin work for you.

What is that railing for anyways? Danny Fuenzalita sees no other way around another useless barrier on the sidewalk of life.

Street titan. Unmatched in his crisp innovative boardwork and creativity, Rodney Mullen only needs a few square feet of EMB stage to rip, but his skating has influenced the scene for miles.

San Francisco skaters eventually troweled ready mix concrete to form a transitioned bowl among a ring of barricades on the city waterfront. Marcus crooked grinds either way.

Knock knock? It's Josh Kalis, passing overhead and over rail from off a downhill snap.

pot check. "New Spots" do come up everyday when you ride a skateboard. Ibon Marino cleans a rugged gap in textbook fashion at the latest gift from the city of San Francisco.

Mark Gonzales does the tailfin slide, in the rain, that was heard 'round the world from Willamette, Oregon.

A little goes a long way. Quim Cardona ollies the small bump at Fort Miley in San Francisco's Presidio and makes it stale and shifted.

All terrain. Bridging the gap between street and vertical skating, Noah Peacock sticks to a city wall and eyes his line for the pedestrian sidewalk slalom and the ensuing high speed hill bomb beyond. Just another typical run down to the corner store in "the biggest skatepark in the world"—San Francisco.

Paid in full. John Cardiel owes nothing in dues and doesn't think about his bank account when trying to conquer new challenges like a kinked rail on Pot Hill in San Francisco. **Results:** Cards: one ad photo, no cover, possible concussion. Railing: still a virgin at last report.

Get there before it's gone. *Thrasher* receptionist Jen Franks spied this spot from the bus to work one morning. Crews were dispatched, mounted on soft red "Krypto" wheels to traverse the flesh-eating finish of what turned out to be an earthquake-proof skyscraper foundation excavation. Who would have known about this site, except skaters like Toad (**left**) and Justin Strubing on night watch.

Natas Kaupas banks to grind while on
patrol through the back lots and alleys
of West L.A.

Fully tubed. Jesse Martinez watches Kelly Jackson work a section amongst a grove of full pipes in Westchester, CA.

Fence jumpin' time. The U.S. Army Corps of Engineers has no competition when it comes to building skate terrain, and they like to keep their secrets. Only skateboarders would brave to obtain the maps and test the waters.

I'd love to meet the first guy who rode a skateboard in a pipe. I wonder what he was thinking when he saw the master cylinder. You think he even got halfway? What made him walk into the abyss in the first place? Do you think he checked out his dust tracks left on the wall and thought it was some form of ancient art? Did he stumble upon it or did he have a mission to do so? What, where, how, and why are significant historical pipe ponderings.

I do know Pat "Muckus" Mullus supposedly found Mt. Baldy pipe and "the line" in the great Aquarian year of 1969. With all of the chaos around the world at that point in time, it is hard to fathom all the monumental happenings made possible by skateboarding in a pipe; turning a negative into a positive, the inverted feeling of the curvaceous conduit carve lines, the adrenaline rush of the dark tunnel sensation, and the echoey chamber of noise only made from a skateboard rolling over a cement structure meant for an entirely different purpose. Like pool riding, pipe riding has adapted like a bastard son of Darwin's survival of the fittest theory—by applying and modifying the original intent specifically made to carry water from point A to point B to a completely radical yet seemingly natural progression of adjusting the astral plane on which to roll upon instead of the usual flat land associated with sidewalk surfing. Call it innovation or what you will—skateboarding is and always will be seeking more sloped, banked, steeper curvy somethings to ride upon or roll over. So what did Mullus do when he saw Baldy for the first time? He freaked and screamed at the top of his lungs, exhilarated by the sights, sounds, and vibes that the place produced. He was also very high . . . on life.

Muck claims that there is a certain cosmic karma involved in tunnel riding and in fact he says, "Pipe riding is medicating for the soul." Pat will forever be the catalyst for something bigger than he could have ever imagined, inspiring hordes of pipe riders who should be thankful and grateful that he found Baldy pipe in the first place.

Mellow Cat was one of the first people to perpetuate the Muckus/Baldy Pipe legend, recreating the myth into the fictional accounts of comic book reality for *Skateboarder* magazine. Was it real or just a figment of one's imagination? Waldo, Mike Weed, Lee Gahimer, Buddy Allred, the Worm, Tom Inouye, and a few others believed. Well, it was real, and Stan Hoffman realized the cylindrical pipe's fatal attraction early on by taking investigative field trips to Baldy for the monumental assurance of building a huge twenty-footer in his historical skatepark, aptly named the Pipeline, inspired of course by the near location and legendary status of Baldy Pipe. Build it and they will come happened way before the movie *Field of Dreams*.

They did come. The pros, the groms, the heshers, moms and pops, school boys and girls, the new kids on the block, and the media. They flocked to the pipe at Pipeline like Indians to a pow wow. They came from all over the world to capture the insane fear and excitement of doing something for the first time in history.

Remember, nobody had done this yet . . . it was all made up only thirty-some years ago, not very long judging by the great cycle of time. Pipe riding, the way we understood it, started right in our backyard of the Badlands at Baldy Pipe, then came into its own at the Pipeline park. More and more pros came to scope out the real deal, and as the word spread, people started looking for more similar stuff.

With practicioners taking pipe riding to new scales and heights, the legends of Baldy and Pipeline became blasé; not because the spots lacked anything spiritually or physically but because pipe riders wanted another kick that allowed them to attain new achievements and new places to explore. With the ushering in of a new age of riders, secret spots and undeterred individualism, pipe riding flourished early on in skating's heyday. Rumors and speculation ruled the telephone wires, and letters of correspondence exchanged ideas, pictures, and maps to the new skate commandos. More and more pipes popped up all over the Western states with Arizona setting the pace from the directorate of Jimmy Carter's great water expansion plan, making it possible for the parched land of the desert near Phoenix to grow economically, agriculturally, and exponentially for the planned business ventures of tomorrow made today. With this newly sought info, pipe riders looked near and far for an adventure that never ceased to amaze.

Meanwhile, up north, Rick Blackhart and the Thatcher bros found out about the Glory Hole and Bombora, two of the most famous pipes ever ridden in the NorCal configuration. The Glory Hole was built in the 1930s; I heard that the pipe was made so big (thirty-two feet I would say) that it swallowed people whole. The pipe is old, leaky, and slightly rough from the wooden slat construction process, but highly recommended for all. A must for anybody who considers themselves to be a pipe guru.

Bombora was a flood control channel that happened to be off of a major highway near the bottom of the bay. Measuring at about eighteen feet, the pics from this place tell the stories of long forgotten riders who accidentally stumbled across it in a rain storm one night. Their car crashed off the side of the embankment and much to the amazement of the banged-up passengers (who luckily got away unscathed), the conduit was fifty feet away from the wreck. Truth is stranger than fiction.

With this said and done, and the concurrent dawning age of skateboarding, bowl/pool contests skaters united all over America in 1978/79 and started coordinating trips to the most desolate places looking for that certain kind of tube ride. Places like Ameron plants and pipe manufacturing places were put on skater's lists of favorite spots to skate. Wind tunnels became the playgrounds of rich, wealthy NASA engineer's sons, who would sneak in after hours much to the delight of their skating friends. Grain silos where everywhere in the Midwest, and all you had to do was find one not standing up. Anything that resembled a pipe or tunnel was fair game to skaters, big or small.

Arizona had Super Tubes, Salt River, Bisquit Flats, Tortilla Mountain, Diablo Mountain, Florence, and others I've forgotten; these were the smoothest things anybody could have ridden. Water projects galore. All Ameron-made, these babies were completely flaw-free, made on sight with special space-age looking technology. Row after row of 22-foot pipes were lined up side by side ready for the taking. Everybody who was anybody in the skate world then skated these pipes. I got to skate every one of these projects since the time I was a kid, and I'm basically the only guy left from all of the people who still jonze for the pipes of the desert. I guess you had to have been there.

Next on the list of skateable super tubes is the big one south of El Paso in the Diablo Lobo mountain range, probably the best thing I've ever skated in my life. Complete with an elbow, this superstructure was built for another purpose, yet somehow skaters found the place in which to practice their craft. Found by locals of Mexican descent, this place is almost as legendary as Baldy pipe—if not more.The 28-foot diameter makes for killer thrill-rides through the darkness and the flat wall is quite sickening, if you ever get to visit this place. Bring lots of water, because the average daily temperature is over 100 degrees from early spring to fall. Maybe you could trade some product for some nice Mexican serapes, but watch the locals—they're hellbent.

Nukeland in San Ofore was another great find, but you had to have military clearance to even get on the land where these babies stood, proudly waiting for a skater's caress. Made for the nuclear power plant, these 18-footers were to be put in the ocean to cool the reactors off. Complete Star Wars secrecy surrounded the project, which was listed under the umbrella of national security/defense. Armed guards stood watch over these precious tubes 24/7, but could be bribed from time to time to take perimeter walks that would last for over two hours. The only reason Cassimus got into Nukeland so many times was that his brother was a Camp Pendleton base commander. How's that for the inside scoop!

Another completely ludicrous place is Pipa Grande, a place kept secret for over twenty years. Tim Puimarta always told me of some lost pipe that Bob Skinner of Haut fame had under his belt. I had heard rumors forever about this place, and when it finally happened (with permission from the caretakers of course), I was away in Norway with Rob Roskopp doing demos in the Arctic Circle. It took me a whole year to set it up again through a friend of a friend. Nightmare to get it going, but a blessing to skate it. Twenty-three feet of pure joy, complete with elbow and flatwall to boot. Another glorious find for mankind, and especially skateboarding in general. Too bad the El Niño floods washed the place away with mudslides from hell. It was so bad that a CHP officer was killed when the whole highway got taken away with muddy water, trees, brush, rocks, and all the other devastating stuff Mother Nature can dish out on a whim. It took two whole years just to fix the highway alone, and the U.S. government decided it would be too costly to ever fix the pipe. So much for that place. . . .

Some people say I have tunnel vision. So be it. I've been riding pipes now since 1975; those were the Glory Days of skating when big pipes were easily accessible, which just isn't the case anymore. I really wish I had the means to skate more pipes, but I'm afraid those days are gone and lost forever. It is definitely a lost art—primitive at its core, yet simplistic and basic in its approach . . . and deadly if you're not careful. Technique is everything in a pipe; the pumping, the glide, the tuck, the sliding and thrusting, the re-direct, the bottom turn, the lines you take, how many kickturns you do per section, how you exit onto the flatwall, how you carve the elbow, and how you handle your speed are all very important factors in being a good pipe rider. You gotta have balls, wits, stamina, endurance, and the will to throw yourself down onto the concrete from at least fifteen feet up if you get pitched; I'm quite sure that anybody who has crushed their bodies slamming in a pipe

will understand completely. What is the adage, "no pain-no gain?" Is the pipe dream gone now, forever vanished and forgotten like yesterday's news? Ya never now what waits up around the bend . . . just when I thought it was all over comes a skatepark out of Canada that has built a 30-foot pipe just for skating, the first one to be built in over twenty years. How do you like them apples? Go smoke another pipe for me, will ya?

—Salba, April 2001

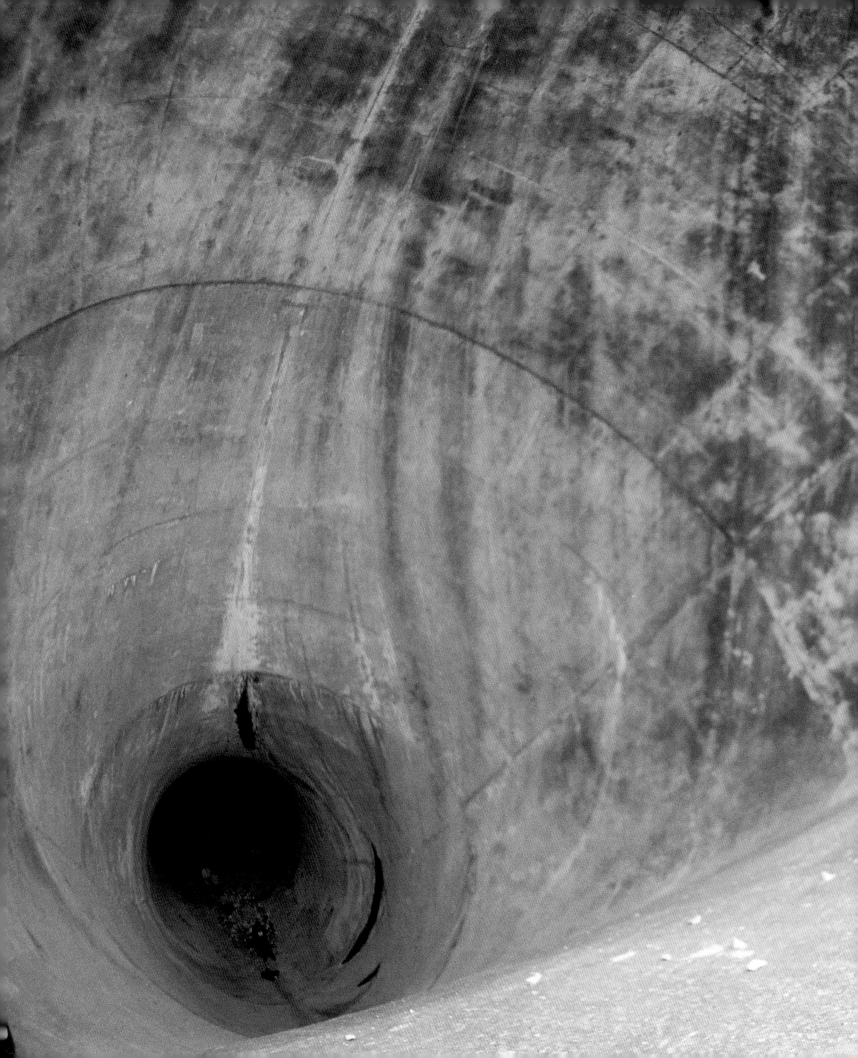

What a way to go. Someday, someone will take the ultimate drop-in at Pipa' Grande in Central Cali. The few skaters who have even ventured to perch themselves at the spillway lip inevitably end up debating which line to take—straight bomb it or corkscrew the roof.

## SECRET SPOTS

Searching through our secret files we found an account of this spot, discovered years ago when roving bands of skate dogs explored the countryside in search of skateable terrain. The file is sprinkled with the names of such notables as Greg "Queaver" Ayres, Doug "Schneidly" Schneider, Rodd "Come up, brah" Saunders and "the Rubber Man" Rick Blackhart. Although the instructions for uncovering the long-hidden map to this secret spot were written in Hindu, the task of deciphering this information was made much easier by our resident guru, who traded his valuable talents for a satchel of rare herbs indigenous to the Northern California coast. Our logistics experts handled preparations for the pilgrimage while our urban band of terrorists employed boats, pontoons, and other strategic materials in their assault of this holy ground. Upon reaching our destination, the mystical experience overcame several of the pale-faced urbanites who were saved from certain dementia by a plunge into the frigid waters of the nearby lake. Once the altar was erected and the holy rituals performed by our fully robed guru, the frenzied skaters proceeded to shred the shrine. No sooner had we consumed the first pack of incense when a frightening flash totally engulfed the sacred spot. We quickly grabbed whatever was in our proximity and split.

Days later, as we recounted our adventure to a group of locals, we realized that our mystical advisor was last seen doing a Bert at 11 o'clock.

—Dudley Counts
January, 1981

Journey to the center of the Earth. Eric Joy digs deep to find the smoothest walls inside Pipa Grande.

King of the Badlands and the Great Lord of pool and pipeology, Steve Alba still plays the flat walls at the mouth of Baldy Pipeline like no other and crosses "the line" beyond where even grafitti can't reach. Salba now makes his home in Ontario, California, gateway to the "Inland Empire" (a developer's term for paved desert), just down the Arrow highway from the ruins of the Upland Pipeline Skatepark and at the center of a fifty-mile circle of sprawl that encompasses more prime pool, pipe, park, drainage, and street terrain than the rest of the earth combined.

lory be. Folklore has it that only two people have died at Glory Hole and neither were skaters. One woman got sucked down in a little rowboat and another person tumbled down the rock face and as slammed to death at the mouth.

Craig Johnson testing and inspecting the flat wall outside the mouth of the Ammo pipe.

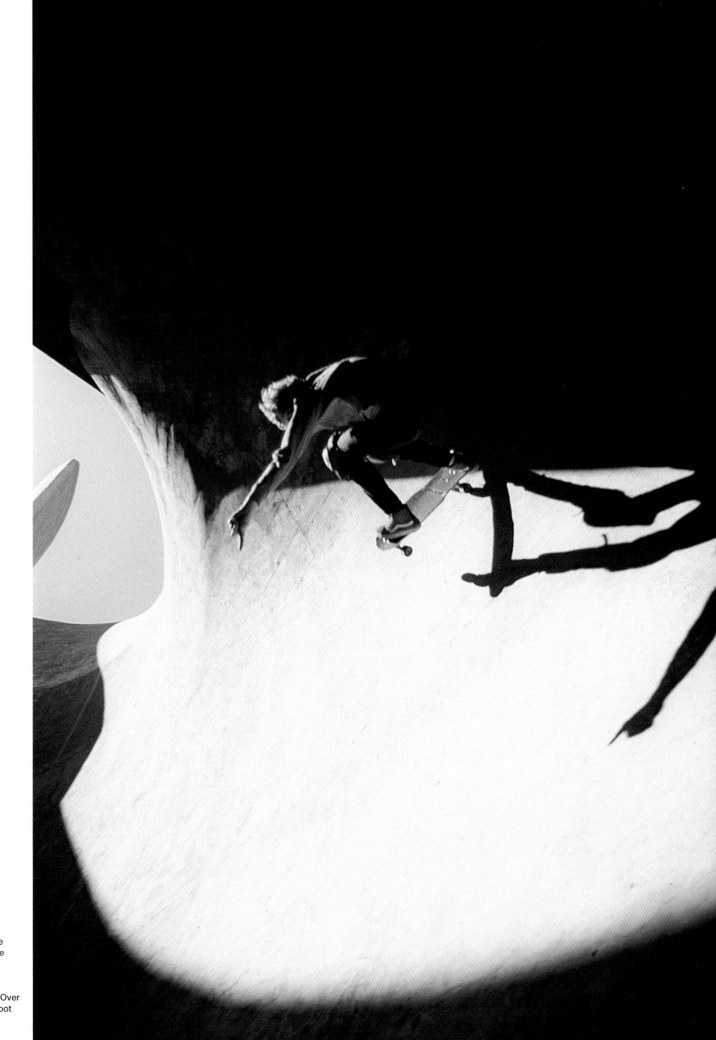

Messin' with Texas. Typifying the Lone Star big and tall skate-style John "Tex" Gibson attacks the upper quadrants of the Ammo Pipe's cathedral-like elbow with respectful and unhurried grace. Over amp here and it's a seventeen-foot space walk back down to earth.

God's a-hole. All terrain champion John Cardiel is beyond the point of no return and still climbing past vertical. Once you start clocking in towards 10:30 the cost of trying to make it is cheaper than the damages if you bail.

Reigning it in. George Orton took many full body slams while launching his patented frontside airs out of the wrong side of Upland's pipe. Pipeline's deep terrain served as proving ground for vert jocks for more than fifteen years but served up many skaters with career-ending body damage.

Land of the Giants. A behemoth cylinder "somewhere in the Southwestern desert." If the skater standing at the mouth is just under six feet tall then the massive maw of the giant Texas tube might be pushing thirty-five feet. This is one of two photos of the only known session there in 1978.

Going underground. Alan Petersen
ollie falls from the roof at Glory Hole.

# TERRAIN OF THE INSANE

Man, during his productive stages, tends to redecorate the world with curious structures. By taking a transient, sometimes irrational, or utopian idea and turning it into a concrete perm, he leaves his mark on the world. Sometimes these ideas pay off, leaving an accomplishment of dubious achievement—form following function. Other times, these finished products serve their purpose but lie in state for many years, sometimes decades, between uses. Of course many fresh ideas just grow old, leading to abandonment, yet the cost of deconstruction in modern dollars can be as high as that which built it yesteryear. It is many of these structures that the skaters of the world seek out and call their own. Discovery of a forgotten spot leads the skateboarder to hours of the good life. For it is they who are capable of seeing the real beauty in the slopes and surfaces of these concrete creations. And when it comes to

riding such "natural terrain," each session provides insight into the irony of what constitutes perfectly skateable terrain. For, as always, those places not intended for skateboarding always seem better than the terrain specifically conceived for the board (*i.e.,* skateboard parks).

A secret skate spot never stays that way for very long and many of the large and legendary skate places are not all that secret to begin with. It may be right in front of your face, or under your feet. You may have even touched it already. Other times, a well known (and watched) swimming pool, spillway or twenty-stair block suddenly becomes available. One thing you can always bet on is that skaters will maximize any opportunity that comes their way. Yet while the attitude is Skate & Destroy, the credo is "Take nothing but pictures (or video), leave only grinds." Or, "one good session deserves another."

Conquered. John Cardiel's expression tells the story as he's all over this long nose slide on a steep California street stair ledge that few had even thought of attempting.

**Previous Spread:** The Seattle Hat is a novelty spot that has been busted on and off for years. Does anybody know if it survived the earthquake of 2001?

Pool with pop. Eric Nash's ollie to tail grab out of the Jelly Bean Bowl proves that a small corner of any yard could host some dynamic skate terrain.

Dinosaur Country. Get-A-Way Skatepark in Huntsville, AL, was another seventies skatepark that barely saw its day before it was demolished.

liding the fall-line of an endless New Mexico ditch, 1990.

**Above:** Peter Hewitt taps out of the pipe end where the fun really begins.

**Right:** Club Med for the Hell-ride crew. Viva Quito, Ecuador, for designing a sick skatepark that doubles as a flood channel and is a sure lure for those nomads who would go to the ends of the earth to wheel its curves.

**Following Spread:**
**Left:** Loop of death. End of the day, several skaters had already been carried out on stretchers when Bob Burnquist charged the made for TV attraction in Tampa, FL, switchstance, nailed it, and sent everyone home.

**Right:** Overview of a one-use contest contraption dubbed the "hellbow," used for the NSA traveling road show contest series in the late eighties.

**This Page and Facing Page:** Skatopia. Rising out of the middle of the Arizona desert, the huge sister sections that formed the Love Bowl were a rumor realized for these roaming skate gypsies.

**Previous Spread:** If there's a God . . . Mere mortals, and cops, look down as they shuffle through their ordinary lives . . . skaters look up, for though they may have sinned, they roll on higher ground.

## TALL TALES
### By Brian Brannon

"Once upon a time, there was a hole in the ground. Some said it was put there by a concrete meteorite. It had huge vertical walls that went up about forty or fifty feet. Most skaters climbed down into it on a worn and weathered garden hose that dangled from the top. No one knew if or when it would break, but we all figured that if it did, it would be a good place to die. We called her the Leisure Bowl, because she was located near an old fart's home called Leisure World. Things were different then. Us kids had respect for our elders, unlike you sniveling punks.

That pool had at least seventy-five feet of vert, but that didn't stop us from shredding tiles. One guy did a knee slide from the top and by the time he was done, both his kneepads and most of his knees were slid clean away. But we never let any minor injuries like that get in our way, no siree, Bob. That's the way it was back then. No tears, no fears. None of this skate-or-die stuff. It was skate-and-die. If you couldn't park two semi-trucks with trailers in it, it was too tight. If you could drop a stone and hear it hit bottom, it was too shallow. Tubes, boobs, and doobs. Them was our main concerns.

You kids talk about your half-pipes and your quarter-pipes, but I ain't seen no ramp that was one-tenth as big as the pipeline I used to skate up north, barefoot. Boy Hardy, was that ever a rat bone to find. The only way you could even get in to that region of country was by mule. Then you had to kayak through rapids and over waterfalls, and after that machete you way through ten miles of thick jungle. If the natives didn't get you, and you could sneak past the giant jungle bunny, you was home free. All you had to do then was scale a 300-foot cliff. It was worth it, though. We called it Bury-us-ahh, 'cuz we decided that was where we would wanted to lay our bones to rest. Of course, youz all know this wasn't exactly legal. There were no membership cards and no Kool-Aid and cookes from Mom when we were done.

Quite a few skaters were missing in action from those places. An ex-con used to sneak around and do in whoever he caught unawares. He has eighteen tears tattooed on his cheeks. One for each dude he murdered. The FBI and the CIA were the only lawmen who ever could have caught us though, believe you me. One time thirty-five police cruisers, twelve unmarked vehicles and four helicopters surrounded the scene of the skate. It was a tough fight, but we beat 'em."

"Ahh, that's horse pucky, Uncle Joe," says a snotty-nosed runt.

"No siree, sonny boy, I'm tellin' it to you straight, just like a Dutch Uncle. Here, come sit on my kneepad."

"Ya see, the reason we overcame them there police was because we had ourselves a secret weapon by the name of Big Bob. It took eighteen officers to hold him down, and when he flexed his stomach, boy, they flew off of him like buckshot from a twelve-gauge. Big Bob was so big that he had to wipe his ass with a bale of hay. Speaking of big things, let me tell y'all about the Monster Bowl. That pool was so long it took twenty minutes of hard pushing just to cover the shallow end. Then you sped down towards the deep end for about forty-five seconds, where you could spend up to five minutes carving the face wall. It took so much water to fill up the Monster Bowl that every summer the Pacific Ocean lost seven feet.

Another fine piece of vert was the Love Bowl. It was a movie set where they used to film them there talking pictures. It had two half-bowls set about fifty yards apart from each other. Both were about thirty feet tall, with twenty feet of vert, and rested on huge turn-tables that allowed you to swivel 'em according to wind direction and available light. I used to pull lien airs to tail from one to the other.

Nope, they don't make 'em like they used to. They don't skate 'em like they used to, neither. Today, to have balls means to ride a particular brand of wheels. Course, there are some good ol' spots still around. Some of them are too dang big to ever get rid of.

Did I ever tell y'all about the time I dropped in at Hoover Dam?"

Gone, but not forgotten. While the abused and loafed ledges of San Francisco's legendary EMB should have been declared a free skate zone, instead, local merchants called skaters "vandals" and the city parked a cop car in the otherwise ugly and neglected plaza. It was a battle made moot when 'barco was later bulldozed and accidently redesigned as an even better spot to chase skaters, while BMX'ers and in-liners wax the ledges.

# SKATE TO THE FUTURE

**Following Spread:** Classic California sillhouette. Rick Blackhart skates off into the sunset at Uvis Dam, 1994.

# THRASHER

THRASHER

SCOOP:

# FUTURE
# SKATEBOARDS

04
APRIL
1991
U.S.
$2.95
CAN.
$3.95

0 102027 4

## INDEX TO PHOTOGRAPHY